Always Read the Leaflet

Getting the best information with every medicine

Report of the Committee on Safety of Medicines
Working Group on Patient Information

Medicines and Healthcare products Regulatory Agency
Committee on Safety of Medicines

London: The Stationery Office

Published by TSO (The Stationery Office) and available from:

Online
www.tso.co.uk/bookshop

Mail, Telephone, Fax & E-mail
TSO
PO Box 29, Norwich, NR3 1GN
Telephone orders/General enquiries: 0870 600 5522
Fax orders: 0870 600 5533
E-mail: book.orders@tso.co.uk
Textphone 0870 240 3701

TSO Shops
123 Kingsway, London, WC2B 6PQ
020 7242 6393 Fax 020 7242 6394
68-69 Bull Street, Birmingham B4 6AD
0121 236 9696 Fax 0121 236 9699
9-21 Princess Street, Manchester M60 8AS
0161 834 7201 Fax 0161 833 0634
16 Arthur Street, Belfast BT1 4GD
028 9023 8451 Fax 028 9023 5401
18-19 High Street, Cardiff CF10 1PT
029 2039 5548 Fax 029 2038 4347
71 Lothian Road, Edinburgh EH3 9AZ
0870 606 5566 Fax 0870 606 5588

TSO Accredited Agents
(see Yellow Pages)

and through good booksellers

First published 2005

ISBN 0 11 703409 6

Printed in the United Kingdom for The Stationery Office
180613 C6 7/05

CONTENTS

FOREWORD

As policy makers and service providers work to increase the amount of choice people can exercise about their healthcare, it is worth remembering that medicine-taking is an area in which people have always made choices and decisions. The act of prescribing or recommending a medicine does not guarantee that it will be taken as advised, for as long as advised, or even at all. These are decisions people make for themselves every day.

This is as it should be. Nobody should ever be expected to take a medicine against their better judgement. What is essential, though, is that the decisions people make about medicines should be informed ones. Given the welter of communications amid which we live, they are all too likely to be based on partial reports, rumour, subliminal advertising and the like.

Survey findings tell us that people want more medicines information than they get[1], that they want it from a range of sources[2], and that they value the patient information leaflet (PIL) more highly than any other source except doctors and pharmacists[2]. PILs are there with the medicine when it is actually being used, and the information they contain is produced by the manufacturer and regulated by law. Therefore they are both easily available and authoritative. Unfortunately they are also often of poor quality and hard to understand.

---

[1] Survey findings:

MORI Research sponsored by Medicines Partnership. Medicines and the British 2003, The Public and Prescribed Medicines 2004;

Schoen C, Osborn R, Huynh P T, Doty M, Davis K, Zapert K & Peugh J. Primary Care And Health System Performance: Adults' Experiences In Five Countries. Health Aff (Millwood) October 2004; and

Healthcare Commission Patient Survey Report 2004: primary care and adult inpatients.

[2] MORI Research sponsored by Medicines Partnership. Medicines and the British 2003, The Public and Prescribed Medicines 2004.

The Patient Information Working Group therefore has its work cut out. Highlights of our first year's work include recommending the early implementation in the UK of mandatory user testing, developing guidance for marketing authorisation holders on this, on usability and on the communication of risk, and considering the special needs of people for whom the leaflet in its standard form is not readily accessible. These have been significant steps forward though there is much more to do. In choosing and tackling these priorities the combined expertise of all my colleagues on the Working Group has been invaluable; we are grateful also to the patient organisations that participated in our first consultation (the first of many, we hope), as well as to the MHRA staff who have supported our work.

Melinda Letts
Chair of the CSM Working Group on Patient Information

EXECUTIVE SUMMARY

Even in this information rich society, the only information many people have about their medicines is the patient information leaflet (PIL) which has been provided with all medicines since 1999. These provide the essential information which patients need to enable them to use the medicine safely and gain the most benefit. Unlike other sources of information, the patient information leaflet is highly regulated. The information to be provided within it is set out in European and national legislation. All patient information leaflets are required to be reviewed and approved by the Medicines and Healthcare products Regulatory Agency (MHRA) before being supplied with the medicine. Whilst basic regulatory requirements are met, the quality of the information is generally seen to be variable. Recent developments have highlighted the growing need for patients to be able to access high quality information about their medicines.

The Committee on Safety of Medicines (CSM) has expressed disquiet over the variable quality of the statutory information and this was supported by views proffered by other organisations such as the Consumers' Association and the National Audit Office[1]. Following the successful review of medicines labelling and the publication of guidance for industry on best practice, the CSM considered that a Working Group on Patient Information should be set up to address these concerns and to champion improvements to PILs.

The full remit is discussed within the report but, in summary, the Group was asked to cover three main areas of work:

- to advise on a strategy to improve the quality of information provided with medicines within the regulatory environment in order to meet patients' needs;

- to propose criteria against which the quality of patient information can be assessed to assure the safe and appropriate use of the medicine and the process by which these will be monitored;

- to advise on key cases which could impact significantly on public health and which will set standards for other products.

All the Group's work has focused on strategies to improve the quality of information provided with medicines within the regulatory environment in order to meet patients' needs. This report summarises the Group's achievements in the following areas:

Patient involvement – recognising the Agency's wish to ensure that all its work on regulating medicines puts the needs of patients at the centre, the Group set a priority on consulting patients. In a new venture for the Agency, a meeting was held to seek the views of representatives from patient, carer and voluntary organisations on PILs and, specifically, on the risk communication proposals.

Quality of PILs – changes in European law affecting PILs have provided an opportunity to make significant improvements, particularly the new requirement that PILs are tested with target users, and changes to the order of information. To take full advantage of these changes, a guideline on user testing of PILs has been developed (Annex 5). New guidance on the usability of PILs sets out principles to ensure they are easily accessible and comprehensive (Annex 6).

Risk communication – information about risk is often not well communicated to the public. The Group has tackled this important topic as it relates to information about taking medicines. The Group evaluated a range of ideas and has made proposals on including headlines and information on the benefits of taking the medicine and specific advice on presenting information about side effects (Annex 9). A guideline on providing information on risk is published for consultation with this report (Annex 10). Leaflets on understanding the risk of side effects with medicines have also been piloted and will be published by the MHRA.

Accessibility of information about medicine taking – the information provided in a PIL is not readily accessible to all patients to meet their needs for information about safe and appropriate use of their medicines. The Group has considered how populations with special needs could be enabled to access this information. They have also considered what additional measures are needed for medicines for children and young people and in situations where medicine taking may be facilitated by a carer. A portfolio of 'information keys' has been developed to aid companies in responding to these needs (Annex 6).

In taking forward this work, the Working Group was mindful of the various stakeholders who had an interest in this area and the output reported aims to address many and varying needs.

Regulatory needs - as a result of the work of the Group, the pharmaceutical industry, which prepares and produces these important documents, is provided with clear guidance on how the regulatory requirements can be met while at the same time answering the information needs of medicine users and carers.

Patients' needs - the patient is seen as vital in the development of the PIL, particularly with the new legal obligations being placed on companies to consult patients to ensure that the resulting document is clear, legible and easy to use. Mechanisms for involving patients are discussed and addressed.

Public awareness - public perception of the patient information leaflet and awareness of its existence is also discussed. The report looks particularly at the communication of risk within the PIL, an issue which patients and the public have criticised widely. It also recommends that the lack of awareness of the PIL should be addressed to promote more widely the role and availability of this important source of medicines information.

Impact assessment - for the future, the Group is keen that the impact of all the Group's recommendations should be assessed to determine their effect and will continue its work to achieve this. Possible strategies are discussed in the report.

References

[1] The Consumers' Association
Patient Information – What's the prognosis? 2003
The National Audit Office
Safety, Quality and Efficacy: Regulating Medicines in the UK TSO London 2003

RECOMMENDATIONS

1. The views of patients should be taken into account at all stages in the development of patient information leaflets (PILs). Usable PILs, designed to meet the needs of patients and support safe and appropriate use of medicines must be the aim of all those involved in their preparation - not simply compliance with the law.

2. PILs should be made more usable by taking the opportunities presented by changes in the law to achieve the best possible content and presentation. To support this, new guidance on usability and on how to take account of the outcome of user consultations should be published for producers of PILs.

3. The guidelines on risk communication included in this report should be the subject of wide consultation. In particular, views should be sought on the concepts of improved order and information on side effects, headline information targeting key messages, and short statements on benefits.

4. To promote consistency and clarity in the writing of PILs, a glossary of lay terms for describing side effects should be developed, tested and enlarged over time.

5. There should be more focus on providing information for patients who have difficulty in accessing the information in the usual PIL, or who have particular needs such as those arising from sight loss or poor basic skills.

6. The information needs of children, young people and carers should receive particular attention.

7. The impact of changes in the quality of PILs as a result of this report should be monitored with the aim of continual improvement, and the supporting guidelines periodically reviewed in the light of experience.

8. Further research should be undertaken on how to provide information in PILs that meets patients' needs in today's environment. In particular, this should explore improved communication of risks and benefits, and how information can promote safe and effective use of medicines by people with diverse needs.

9. Options should be explored for improved access to PILs, including availability at or before the prescription or purchase of a medicine, and in other situations where a PIL is not currently available.

10. Steps should be taken to promote wide public awareness of PILs and their availability in alternative formats. These should include publicity about the Group's leaflet on the risks and benefits of medicines.

1 INTRODUCTION AND THE NEED FOR A WORKING GROUP

SUMMARY

People expect and are entitled to good quality information about their medicines, whether prescribed or bought over the counter. Informed decision-making by patients and the public about medicines is keenly promoted by the Department of Health, and is an issue with which healthcare professionals are increasingly becoming familiar. The quantity of medicines information available to today's patients and carers is not in doubt; its quality very often has been. The result has been, at best, confusing for medicine users and, at worst, downright dangerous.

The legal framework covering patient information leaflets (PILs) has been in force for a number of years but the information provided has often failed to meet medicine users' needs. The Consumers' Association in 2003 published a policy report entitled *Patient Information – What's the Prognosis*[1] which looked at all information available to patients. Among other recommendations, the Consumers' Association specifically called for improvements to the statutory PIL. Another report in the same year which drew attention to the variable quality of PILs was the National Audit Office's *Safety, Quality and Efficacy – Regulating Medicines in the UK.*[2] While recognising that improvements had been made, the report recommended more patient involvement in the development of the information and in user testing, and better communication about risks associated with medicine-taking.

The Committee on Safety of Medicines considered these reports in 2003, together with concerns arising from their regular review of the PILs included with applications presented to them. They recommended that a Working Group on patient information should be set up to address concerns relating to the quality of PILs and to champion improvements to patient information leaflets. The Group met for the first time in November 2003 and set as its priorities: risk communication, the quality of information in leaflets, and meeting patients' needs. These are discussed in detail in the following chapters.

1.1 THE ROLE OF THE PATIENT INFORMATION LEAFLET IN AN INFORMATION-RICH SOCIETY

We live in a society rich in information sources. Patients increasingly expect to be able to access information to enable them to make informed decisions about their health. Good information helps patients participate fully in concordant decision-making about the medicines prescribed for, or recommended to, them by health care professionals. Similarly, self-care, a theme running through many Government initiatives including the Expert Patient Programme and the programme for managing long-term conditions, relies heavily on patients having sufficient, high quality information on which to base their decision-making. A significant part of this comes from consultation with a healthcare professional for prescription medicines; however, such advice cannot be relied on as the only source of information for all patients. For medicines purchased over the counter, interaction between the patient and a healthcare professional may be limited or unavailable. Written information then has an increased importance for safe use of the medicine.

There is an enormous amount of information about health and medicines available from many different sources but it is not always easy for patients to access. Nor is it always clear how reliable, authoritative or up to date such sources of information are. The range of sources includes:

- health charities and patient support groups;

- doctors' waiting rooms, pharmacies, hospitals and clinics which frequently display leaflets about medicines and disease states which have been distributed in partnership with professional bodies;

- the internet and the media which carry information about medicines and health, although the usefulness of such information can be variable.

Even so, many patients lack access to information which others in society take for granted.

For many people, the primary or only source of information about their medicine is the statutory patient information leaflets which, since 1999, have had to be supplied with all medicines. These provide the essential information which patients need to enable them to use medicines safely and gain the most benefit. Unlike other sources of information, the patient information leaflet is highly regulated. All PILs are required to be reviewed and approved by the Medicines and Healthcare products Regulatory Agency before being supplied with the medicine. The information which is provided within the PIL is set out in European and national legislation. Whilst basic regulatory requirements are met, the quality of the information has generally been seen to be variable.

1.2 WHY PATIENT INFORMATION LEAFLETS NEED IMPROVEMENT

The legal framework covering PILs has been in force for a number of years, but often the information provided has failed to meet patients' needs. The Consumers' Association (now known as Which?) in 2003 published a policy report entitled *Patient Information – What's the Prognosis?* [1] which took an across the board look at all information provided, including the statutory PIL. The report highlighted the need for high quality patient information from trusted sources; it stressed the need to design the information around the patient, and one recommendation specifically called for improvements to the existing statutory PIL.

Also in 2003, the National Audit Office (NAO) published its report *Safety, Quality and Efficacy – Regulating Medicines in the UK.* [2] This too drew attention to the variable quality of PILs. Although the report recognised that significant improvements had been achieved over the years, it acknowledged that much more could be achieved within the current regulatory framework to enhance the quality of the information provided with medicines. The NAO recommended that improvements could be achieved by involving patients much more in the development of the information. It recognised that a key concern for patients was the way in which the risks associated with medicine-taking were described in terms which were not helpful to patients, and that this could be addressed by making sure PILs were tested with patients prior to supply.

These reports, the perception of members of the Committee on Safety of Medicines, and complaints to the MHRA all criticised the quality of the information provided as not meeting patients' needs. A number of factors contributed to this:

- the order in which this information must appear, a legal requirement, was unhelpful;

- the leaflet must reflect the product licence (the Summary of Product Characteristics (SPC)) of the product to which it refers. Differences between the SPCs for the same medicine available from different MA holders led to inconsistent information in the PIL, resulting in frequent complaints from patients;

- many leaflets were lengthy due to the complexity of the SPC, and were poorly laid out. Patients quickly lost interest in the document, failing to read or understand information crucial to the safe use of the medicine;

- perhaps the most significant criticism of the information contained within the PIL related to poor communication of risk. Published studies indicated that patients' understanding of terms commonly used by healthcare professionals generally exaggerated the likelihood of risk [3];

■ although user testing had been part of the EC guidance available to MA holders, few companies recognised the importance of seeking the views of patients on the information they provide and little, if any, user testing had been undertaken.

All of these issues taken together created the potential for confusion and lack of trust by the patient. Many PILs which could be a useful communication tool became yet another wasted opportunity for informing and educating.

1.3 ESTABLISHING A WORKING GROUP OF THE COMMITTEE ON SAFETY OF MEDICINES

The Committee on Safety of Medicines has taken a close interest in the developments relating to patient information leaflets over the years and has often expressed concern that quality improvements have not been taken forward more rapidly. In the spring of 2003, following the review of medicines labelling and the publication of guidance for industry on best practice, the CSM considered all the issues in relation to PILs and set up a Working Group on Patient Information to address these concerns and to champion improvements to PILs.

The CSM discussed and agreed the proposed remit of the Group. This is provided at Annex 2. In essence, the purpose of the Group was to consider how the quality of the information provided with medicines could be improved and to produce guidance for those involved in the writing of the patient information leaflet. The goal was high quality PILs which promote safe and effective use of medicines. In summary, the Group was asked to cover three main areas of work:

■ to advise on a strategy to improve the quality of information provided with medicines within the regulatory environment in order to meet patient needs;

■ to propose criteria against which the quality of patient information can be assessed to assure the safe and appropriate use of the medicine, and the process by which these will be monitored;

■ to advise on key patient information leaflets which could impact significantly on public health and which will set standards for other products.

Members of the Working Group were appointed for their expertise in patient information and were drawn from a variety of backgrounds including patient and consumer organisations, academia and industry. Melinda Letts, immediate past chair of the Long-term Medical Conditions Alliance, was appointed to the chair. A list of the members of the Group and their interests is provided at Annex 1.

1.4   SETTING PRIORITIES

At its first meeting, the Working Group initiated a priority-setting exercise in relation to the current information provisions and their shortcomings. Members considered a number of key topics as a basis for the future work plan of the Group.

Quality of information in leaflets

A major criticism of the current patient information leaflets was that many were considered to be of poor quality. Although involving patients in the development of the leaflet was recommended, it was not a legal requirement. The Group considered that as a priority and, to coincide with the new legislative requirements, greater emphasis should be placed on the involvement of the patient in the writing of the leaflet along with updated guidance on performance-based testing of the PIL prior to marketing. This aspect of the work of the Group is discussed in more detail in Chapter 3.

Risk communication

The Working Group recognised that patients' understanding of risk and the balance of risk and benefit with medicines is variable. Although some limited guidance had been made available in the European regulatory context, the Working Group felt that significant improvements in the way in which risk was communicated within patient information leaflets could be achieved if new guidance was developed. They also recognised that patients needed support to interpret information on risk and that certain key information needed to be clearly understood by patients to ensure that medicines were used safely. They identified as a high priority the need for the development and elaboration of guidance in the area of risk communication and sought to achieve this in advance of changes to the European legislation surrounding patient information. This aspect of the work of the Group is discussed in more detail in Chapter 4.

Meeting patients' needs

The Working Group reviewed the evidence from recent reports that the patient information leaflets currently available did not meet the needs of patients. Often, the leaflet was considered to have little relevance to the patient taking the medicine. They recognised that this was partly due to lack of patient involvement in the writing of the PILs but also considered that there were likely to be particular groups of patients who may have particular information needs. A strand of work was proposed which would consider these issues and propose a way forward. This aspect of the work of the Group is discussed in more detail in Chapter 5.

Patient involvement

The Working Group recognised that at the centre of all its proposed work was the imperative that the information should meet the needs of patients. The Working Group undertook to consult patient, carer and voluntary organisations to ensure that its work focused on the needs of patients. The success of any improvements to patient information leaflets would be measured against this same yardstick.

References

1. Consumers' Association. Patient Information – What's the Prognosis. London. February 2003.

2. National Audit Office. Safety, Quality and Efficacy – Regulating Medicines in the UK. London. January 2003.

3. Berry D C, Raynor D K & Knapp P. Communicating risk of medication side effects: an empirical evaluation of EU recommended terminology. Psychology, Health & Medicine 2003; 8 (No 3): 451-263.

2 HISTORY OF PATIENT INFORMATION IN THE UNITED KINGDOM AND THE LEGISLATIVE FRAMEWORK

SUMMARY

Legislation regulating patient information with medicines has been in place in the UK since 1977. Over the years this has changed and grown. This chapter reviews what has been available to those involved in writing patient information to accompany medicines.

Changes to the European legislation to be implemented in 2005 require companies to consult with target patient groups when developing PILs.   In addition, the order of the leaflet information will be changed so that important safety messages are presented in a more prominent manner. The Group advised that prompt and efficient implementation of these legal changes should quickly lead to better patient information with consequent benefits in public health and enhanced patient safety. Although recognising that marketing authorisation holders would need to make fundamental changes to their procedures, patients' interests were considered by the Group to be paramount.

2.1 BACKGROUND TO THE LEGAL POSITION

Patient information with medicines has been regulated in the United Kingdom since 1977. Although few medicines at that time were supplied with leaflets, those leaflets which were produced had to comply with certain legal requirements.   Medicines which were supplied with leaflets for patients in the 1970s and '80s were usually inhaled medicines and others which required detailed instructions for use by patients self-medicating outside the healthcare environment.

In 1992 the European Commission issued a Directive[1] on the labelling of medicinal products for human use and on package leaflets.   The main purpose of the labelling and patient information leaflet provisions was to give users full and comprehensible information so that medicines could be used safely and effectively.   Patient safety was the over-riding concern and leaflets had to reflect the terms of the marketing authorisation.

This Directive was implemented into UK legislation in 1994[2] and formed the basis for the introduction of patient information leaflets for all medicines over the next five years. By 1999 all medicines on the market had authorised patient information – effectively giving a "window" on the licence information already available to health care professionals. The information had to be set out in a particular order and written in terms which the patient could understand. To help companies meet the new requirements for patient information leaflets, the then Medicines Control Agency produced a guidance document[3] on interpretation of the regulatory position. This guidance informed the subsequent development of guidance[4] from the European Commission. Since then, all the medicines Directives from Europe have been brought together into one codified text.[5]

2.2 THE INFORMATION NECESSARY FOR INCLUSION IN A PATIENT INFORMATION LEAFLET

The legislation requires that the leaflet should be drawn up in accordance with the Summary of Product Characteristics and contain specific pieces of information in a specific order. The Directive prescribed seven sections within the PIL.

- **Identification of the medicine**

  The name, the active substance and details of the other ingredients, the pharmaceutical form, contents within the pack, the name and address of the holder of the marketing authorisation and the manufacturer and the way in which the medicine works.

- **Therapeutic indications for the product**

  The conditions for which the medicine is authorised.

- **Information which patients need to be aware of prior to taking the medicine**

  Situations when the medicine should not be used, any precautions and warnings, interactions with other medicines or foods, special patient populations such as pregnant or nursing mothers, and any effects the medicine may have on the patient's ability to drive.

- **Dosage and usual instructions for use**

  How to take or use the medicine, how often the dose should be given, how long the course of treatment will last, what to do if a dose is missed and, if relevant, the risk of withdrawal effects.

- **Description of side effects**

  All the effects which may occur under normal use of the product and what action the patient should take if any of these occur.

- **How to store the product**

- **Date on which the leaflet was prepared**

Additional information may be included in the leaflet and must be compatible with the SPC, useful for health education and non-promotional. Information about the disease being treated or lifestyle changes which would benefit the patient and details of patient support services can be included under this provision.

The PIL must be written in the official language of the member state (for the UK this is English) although other languages may be used as well, provided that the same particulars appear in all languages used. The document must also be written in clear and understandable terms for the users and be clearly legible.

2.3 NEW LEGISLATIVE AMENDMENTS AND THE OPPORTUNITY FOR CHANGE

Changes to the European legislation made in 2004[6] introduced a new legal obligation on all marketing authorisation holders to ensure that all patient information leaflets reflect the results of consultations with target patient groups (user testing). This provided a major step forward in providing regulators with powers to ensure that the leaflet is legible, clear and easy to use. A separate amendment to the order of the leaflet information ensures that important safety messages are presented in a more logical manner. The information is now re-ordered to ensure that the important safety messages appear nearer the beginning of the document, with full formulation details and companies' addresses now coming at the end. These changes are described in detail in Chapter 3 of this report. The due date for Europe-wide implementation is October 2005.

The Working Group considered that early implementation of these legal amendments in the UK would provide a significant benefit to public health, enhance patient safety and further the Group's long term strategy in relation to quality improvements to patient information. It would also set clear standards on how the new requirements could be met. Although recognising that marketing authorisation holders would need to make changes in their procedures, an over-riding concern was that patients' interests should be paramount. The Group considered that prompt action to implement the new legislation was necessary, and that the benefits of introducing these new provisions early outweighed any contrary views.

The MHRA undertook a public consultation on the proposal to take forward the amendments in the legal provision in advance of the EC deadline[7]. The Group supported these early changes and a copy of their response to the consultation exercise is at Annex 3. A statutory instrument[8] was laid in Parliament in December 2004 to implement the legislative changes in the UK from 1 July 2005. All new applications from that date will have to comply with the new legal requirements, with a three year transitional period for existing products until July 2008.

References

1. European Commission. Council Directive 92/27/EEC on the labelling of medicinal products for human use and on package leaflets. March 1992.

2. The Medicines (Labelling) Amendment Regulations 1992. SI 1992/3273.
   The Medicines (Leaflet) Amendment Regulations 1992. SI 1992/3274.
   The Medicines for Human Use (Marketing Authorisations Etc.) Regulations 1994. SI 1994/3144.

3. MCA Guidance for the Pharmaceutical Industry on the Labelling and Leaflets Regulations. MCA Guidance Note 20. September 1993.

4. European Commission. Guideline on the Readability of the Label and Package Leaflet of Medicinal Products for Human Use. September 1998.

5. European Commission. Directive 2001/83/EC of the European Parliament and of the Council of 6 November 2001 on the Community code relating to medicinal products for human use. November 2001.

6. European Commission. Directive 2004/27/EC of the European Parliament and of the Council of 31 March 2004 amending Directive 2001/83/EC on the Community code relating to medicinal products for human use. March 2004.

7. MHRA. Consultation Letter: MLX 309 - Implementation of revised EU medicines legislation: implementing the "2001 Review". July 2004.

8. The Medicines (Marketing Authorisation and Miscellaneous Amendments) Regulations 2004. SI 2004/3224.

3 INFORMATION PEOPLE CAN USE

SUMMARY

The Group sought advice from patients and experts on the quality of patient information leaflets and priorities for improvement. The Group then prioritised the development of guidance on usability factors which affect the readability of the leaflet and guidelines on user testing to support the introduction of the legal requirement for patient consultation. This chapter describes the key principles identified to promote improvements to the quality of PILs. These have been developed into published guidance documents to enable industry to comply with the new legal requirements and produce clear, legible PILs containing information in a form that patients can use.

3.1 WHAT IMPROVEMENTS ARE REQUIRED?

To build on the evidence on PILs discussed in the previous chapters, the Group undertook a series of activities to review the quality of current PILs and obtain advice in order to develop proposals on how they could be improved.

3.1.1 Seeking patients' views

The first priority was to seek the views of patients. This recognised the Agency's wish to ensure that all its work on regulating medicines revolves around patients' needs. In July 2004, as a first step towards involving patients in their work, the Group held a meeting with representatives of patient, carer and other voluntary organisations. This was a new initiative for the Agency to explore how the issues relating to patient information with medicines are perceived by patient groups, and how the needs of patients may be more fully met by information provided with medicines in the future. The Group acknowledges the input from all the organisations consulted in this aspect of their work. A list of patient organisations represented is at Annex 4.

The advice given by the patients' organisations on the quality of patient information leaflets is summarised below:

■ PILs need improvement. Their quality is variable and they often contain complex language and too much jargon;

■ often the leaflet is too busy and the print too small;

■ leaflets are too negative with insufficient information on the benefits of taking the medicine, making it difficult for the patient to assess risk versus benefit;

■ the PIL should supplement discussion with the prescriber. It should be consistent with the advice given and, ideally, be available during the discussion;

■ different patients may have different needs and one PIL would not meet all of these. Information in the PIL about patient organisations where further advice could be obtained would be useful;

■ helpline numbers and website addresses are also useful pointers to further information, and access to these should be made more use of in the PIL;

■ comparative information and information about lifestyle issues can aid patients in their decision making.

The consultation also sought views on the communication of risk, discussed further in Chapter 4. The valuable input from patient representatives reinforced points made in Chapter 1 on issues about the quality of PILs.

3.1.2 Seeking expert views

The Group also heard from members of the Group who had conducted research with patients on the quality of information about medicines in general and PILs in particular. Views were presented on medicines information which was intended to help the patient use the medicine appropriately. One particularly telling quote referred to the way the leaflet was written "That's the medicines language. It's not of any interest to me"[1].

The Group was presented with extracts from leaflets where communication of information was poor and with a model leaflet showing how the information could be presented clearly. These served to highlight the following issues:

■ use of jargon, as in "see your doctor if you suffer from ... non-cirrhotic alcoholic liver disease";

■ use of capital letters - eye-catching but hard to read;

■ inappropriate punctuation - obscures the message;

■ text in boxes - often skipped over;

■ euphemisms such as "Can your tablets upset you?" - not helpful when referring to serious side effects;

■ highlighting important text by use of colour or bold text - can be helpful but overuse loses prominence;

■ the need for messages to be consistent. For example, red warning text at the end of a section of text sends confusing messages as to whether it is important;

■ language - should be clear and unambiguous.

The differences between the views of patients and healthcare professionals on what was important in a leaflet were highlighted. Research[2] has shown that patients prioritise four key points of information about a medicine - side effects, dos and don'ts, what it does and how to take it – but different people prefer different orders of priority.

Recognising that many patients do not read the leaflet for various reasons, it was demonstrated that a short summary of key information could be useful. This could be less off-putting than the full leaflet, meaning that more patients may read the key information. This proposal has been taken forward in Chapter 4.

3.1.3   Case work – lessons learnt

The Group also reviewed a number of patient information leaflets where there were important issues of public safety. By considering these leaflets, the Group was able immediately to set in train quality improvements in line with the ongoing work on risk communication and usability. This aspect of the work also served to inform the Group's wider discussion by using practical examples to identify principles to be incorporated into guidance. Examples of good and poor practice were also identified. The Group concurred with issues raised by the patient groups and the external reports referenced earlier. Key points arising included the following:

■ text size is frequently too small to be easily legible by the majority of patients;

■ the language is often complex and uses medical jargon, alienating patients from the text;

■ communication of risk is frequently poor with few explanations;

■ there can be a lack of balance in the information, resulting in a negative perception on the part of the reader;

■ layout of the information often makes navigation through the leaflet difficult for the average reader;

■ important information is often difficult to locate.

3.1.4 Case work example – Seroxat

At the request of the CSM Expert Working Group on Selective Serotonin Reuptake Inhibitors (SSRIs), the Working Group on Patient Information convened a focus group meeting for representatives from SSRI patient interest and user groups. The focus group sought the views of attendees on whether the proposed PIL for Seroxat (paroxetine) met the needs of users for written information provided with the medicine. The advice of the focus group and the Working Group was provided on the Seroxat PIL as a template or exemplar for PILs for other SSRI products. A report of the Group's discussion is provided at Annex 7.

The focus group participants supported the concept of "headlines" to contain key safety information and warnings about use of the product that a patient needed to be aware of at the start of treatment. They advised that primary warnings to allow patients to make an informed choice in terms of the harm-to-benefit balance should be in larger print at the top of the PIL.

Participants were also concerned that information on benefit should be included to provide a balanced presentation of the treatment. The key messages to support safe use of the product, such as information on taking other medicines and use in pregnancy, should be clear and easy to find. Explanations of the reasons for instructions such as "You should not drink alcohol" were also needed. The group did not find a listing of side effects by frequency to be helpful in identifying particular effects.

More generally, the focus group was concerned that this and other PILs may not be easily understood by patients. They considered that the PILs should be improved by providing information up-front to allow patients to make an informed choice. Leaflets should also make it clear that patients can seek advice if they are unsure.

3.1.5 Development of the patient information leaflet by the pharmaceutical company

The Working Group also considered how statutory patient information leaflets are produced by medicines manufacturers. Although the leaflet is the public face of the medicine, often the company marketing the product did not begin to plan the content of the leaflet until the end of the medicine development process. In the past, little thought has been given to involving patients in the writing and testing of the information. The resulting leaflet has often been a lengthy and technical document which patients are not inclined to read. If they do read it, patients are frequently faced with information which they cannot understand and which leaves them feeling frightened and vulnerable.

As a result, the patient information leaflet, which should be a valuable source of accessible and useful information, vital for the safe and effective use of the medicine, remains in the carton, unread. A huge opportunity for communicating important health messages is lost and patients remain isolated and uninformed.

The Group recognised that there was a missed opportunity here for marketing authorisation holders to engage with patients as early as possible to ensure that, by the time the medicine reached the market place, clear and accessible information had been developed.

3.1.6 Official guidance on PILS

The European Commission has published two guidelines which have impacted on the quality of the information provided. As guidance these documents are advisory only and have no legal force behind them.

▪ Excipients guideline

In 1997 the European Commission published a guideline on excipients (ingredients other than the active substance) which themselves have a recognised effect and which should be the subject of special consideration within the product information. This guideline was revised in 2003[3] and includes simplified warnings for inclusion in the PIL.

▪ Readability guideline

In January 1999 the European Commission published a "Guideline on the Readability of the Label and Package Leaflet of Medicinal Products for Human Use"[4]. The guideline included a protocol for a user test which sets out to demonstrate whether patients can understand the information and use the medicine safely. If the required standard of readability was assured by reference to a leaflet for a similar product where a test had been done, a user test was not required for each individual leaflet.

The readibility guideline also considered those factors which will influence the readability of the PIL. These include the size of the font used, print colour, syntax and the weight of paper used. A minimum font size was recommended but in practice, however, leaflets written in text of this size are too small for many patients to read easily.

The guideline made a number of recommendations to improve readability:

- in compiling the text long sentences should be avoided;

- the length of the line of text should be restricted;

- different fonts should be used, along with upper and lower case lettering;

- punctuation should be light and, where appropriate, bullet points should be used;

- the name of the product should be used sparingly throughout the text;

- the style of writing should be active and direct and the text should be phrased so that it is readily understandable for the patient.

This EC readability guideline has had a significant impact on the quality of the information provided in PILs. As a result, many PILs now contain a better balance of the risks and benefits offered by a particular medicine but there is much more which could be achieved within the current regulatory framework.

3.2 REVIEW OF CURRENT GUIDANCE

Having considered all the evidence summarised above, the Group took the view that the currently available guidance on readability[4] did not reflect current knowledge on the factors which should be taken into account when preparing written documentation about medicines. The Group considered that the readability guideline, although helpful, would benefit from redrafting in a manner which offers those responsible for the preparation of patient information more detailed advice on how best to meet both the regulatory requirements and the growing expectations of patients.

The current guidance is divided into three parts:

- the information to be included and how it should be presented (including a model leaflet);

- design factors which affect the accessibility and readability of the information (usability factors); and

- how to undertake user testing.

The information content is required by European law. The Group recognised that this would not change (although the order would become more logical) and therefore decided that the most important change to improve the information presented was to address the communication of risk. This is discussed in Chapter 4.

To make improvements to quality, progress should be made on new guidance for the remaining two areas of usability factors and user testing. The work of the Group on these is summarised below.

In addition, the Group drew attention to the general advice and guidance on clarity of communication in writing health information available from a number of sources. A selection of key sources of guidance and support is listed at the end of this chapter.

The Group also heard that the MHRA is leading, with the European Medicines Agency, on a Europe-wide review of the readability guideline. The work of the Group in advising on new UK guidance would provide the basis for development of a new European guideline. It is envisaged that there will be a suite of guidance covering the following issues:

- the information to be included in each section;

- usability factors;

- user testing;

- advice on the use of templates and model leaflets.

3.3 DEVELOPING GUIDANCE ON THE FACTORS WHICH AFFECT THE ACCESSIBILITY AND READABILITY OF THE INFORMATION – USABILITY

The Group considered the principles which should be adopted in producing information for patients about medicines. In developing these principles, the Group focused on the factors which assist in producing leaflets which are easy for patients to read. The marketing authorisation holder must ensure that the patient information leaflet is written and designed so that it is clear and understandable to the reader.

The Working Group has developed guidance on usability, provided at Annex 6. This considers in detail the factors which should be addressed when designing and setting out the information required.

Factors which influence the clarity and legibility of the written information were given particular emphasis. In particular, the Group advised on the following.

- **Writing style:** advice is given on choice of words, punctuation and sentence length, short paragraphs and use of bullets to make the text easier to understand.

- **The typeface:** this includes easy-to-read serif-type fonts, restricting the use of capitals, and avoiding italics and underlining to make word recognition easier. A key change is an increase in the recommended text size to ensure more patients are able to read the information provided.

- **Design and layout:** this is key to aiding the reader to navigate around the sections of the leaflet. Principles identified include the need for clear spacing, attention to paragraph length and choice of uncoated paper. Use of column formats was found to be helpful and advice is given on separation of columns and sections and on ensuring that key information is kept together.

- **Headings:** these are important for navigation and should be presented consistently through the document. Use of colour or bold text can help to make headers stand out.

- **Use of colour:** judicious use of colour can aid navigation but attention to contrast is important for readability. Advice is also provided on use of reverse type to highlight key information.

- **Use of symbols and pictograms:** it is essential that the meaning of any symbol is clear and this should always be user tested. It cannot substitute for verbal advice.

The guidance also considered the use of templates to ensure that the information is presented in a consistent manner compatible with the legal requirements, and recognises that these can be helpful to ensure all the information is included. However, these can inhibit innovation in designing and presenting information in ways that patients find accessible.

The guidance has been combined with advice on information keys to meet the needs of special groups of people for whom the PIL in the medicine pack is less useful as a source of information. This is discussed in chapter 5.

Importantly, the guidance document recognises that even taking these factors into account, the information produced will still need to be tested with patients to make sure that the important safety messages within the leaflet are fully understood by the reader. This is discussed in detail below.

3.4 INVOLVING PATIENTS IN PATIENT INFORMATION LEAFLETS

3.4.1 Background

The European Commission Guideline on the Readability of the Label and Package Leaflet of Medicinal Products for Human Use[4] includes within it an example of a user testing method. In drafting that document, the Commission reflected the work of Professor David Sless[5] and considered that diagnostic testing would best demonstrate that patients could find, understand and act upon the safety messages within leaflets. So far very little user testing has been carried out within the UK, although for products centrally authorised for supply in all member states across Europe a user test is recommended, but not required, prior to approval of the leaflet.

As there are no means by which member states can require an applicant to carry out such a test in the absence of a legislative requirement. The desired improvement in quality has not therefore been realised in practice.

Although little formal user testing has been undertaken on patient information leaflets within the UK, where this has been done the resulting information has been of a much higher quality. The results of user testing have demonstrated that patient involvement is key to the production of information leaflets which address the concerns raised by patients themselves and the organisations which campaign on their behalf.

3.4.2 New legal obligations on marketing authorisation holders

As discussed in Chapter 2, new European legislation[6] on PILs is implemented in the UK from July 2005. The most significant change is the amendment to include a requirement that user testing be carried out to demonstrate the readability and usefulness of the PIL to patients. This new provision specifies that:

"The package leaflet shall reflect the results of consultations with target patient groups to ensure that it is legible, clear and easy to use."

25

In addition, there is a further new requirement that products authorised in several Member States through the European mutual recognition and decentralised procedures will have a harmonised PIL (currently this is the position for centrally authorised products only).

The Working Group considered how guidance could advise marketing authorisation holders on how best to engage with patients and meet the legal obligation of consulting with patient groups in developing patient information which is legible, clear and easy to use.

3.5 DEVELOPING GUIDANCE ON USER TESTING OF PATIENT INFORMATION

The introduction of new European legislation provided the Working Group with the opportunity to develop guidance on how patient information should be designed and tested. In developing this guidance the Group drew on the expertise of members* in addition to reviewing previously published work by experts in the field. The consensus document is at Annex 5.

The detailed guidance developed by the Group recognises that a variety of methods may be used to satisfy the legal requirement and uses as an example a suitable method set down in earlier guidance from the European Commission and validated by several years' regulatory experience in Australia. In developing the guidance, the Working Group was concerned to ensure that it provided sufficient advice to companies so that they could understand how they could comply in practice with the legal requirement for user consultation. The proposed test method, however, is not prescriptive and, to support innovation, the guidance clearly recognises that other performance based test protocols are equally valid.

3.5.1 Defining "user testing"

The legislation does not require any particular method of testing to have been used, but the consultations with target patient groups should provide evidence that people who are likely to rely on the leaflet can find and appropriately use the information. Companies are advised to ensure that they have:

- clearly defined before the test what the **most important information** is – for example, what the medicine is for, the dosage and any significant side effects and warnings;

- reflected in the test sample **populations who are particularly likely to rely on the leaflet** for the medicine in question (these may include carers);

■ provided **credible evidence**, for example data gathered from test participants to a clear protocol;

■ provided evidence that test participants can **find and appropriately use the information.**

The Working Group advised that any user test submitted in support of a patient information leaflet needs to address the following issues.

■ Evidence is likely to be composed of data gathered from users under controlled conditions. For example, the evidence from tests on very similar leaflets may be used in a complementary manner.

■ Which people are likely to rely on the leaflet for a particular medicine will depend upon a number of factors, such as whether the medicine is generally intended for administration by someone other than the patient.

■ In order to ensure that those involved can understand and apply the information, the evidence presented must demonstrate that they can pick out the relevant information, interpret this and describe the action they would take as a result.

■ The key information will need to be defined prior to the test by the marketing authorisation holders and is likely to include any significant potential side effects and warnings as well as what the medicine is for and the dosage.

3.5.2   Recruiting participants

The Group advised on how participants could be recruited and the numbers needed to provide adequate assurance that the information meets the criteria set out above. Members considered that a range of different types of people able to imagine needing to use the medicine should be involved. If the medicine is intended for a rare illness, where possible the leaflet should be tested among people with the illness. People who have previously taken, or are currently taking, the medicine should be excluded. Test subjects could include:

■ particular age groups such as young people and older people – especially if the medicine is particularly relevant to their age group;

■ new users or people who do not normally use medicines, particularly for information provided with new medicines likely to be used by a wide range of people (eg analgesics or antihistamines);

■ people who do not use written documents in their working life;

■ people who find written information difficult.

Suitable participants could be recruited from the following organisations:

- older people's lunch clubs;

- self-help groups;

- patient support groups;

- community centres;

- parent and toddler groups.

3.5.3 When to undertake a user test

In considering when user consultation should be undertaken, the Working Group recognised that there will be circumstances when sufficient similarities exist between leaflets that evidence obtained in support of one leaflet could support the writing of related documents. Nevertheless, there will be occasions when user consultation would always be required such as new chemical entities, medicines which have undergone a change in legal status and those with a novel presentation.

3.6 IMPLEMENTING THE GUIDANCE

The guidance on usability and user testing is published with this report. Companies will be expected to take account of the guidance in all applications submitted after the legal changes are implemented in July 2005. It will be important to assess the impact of these changes and the Group made the following recommendations for further work.

RECOMMENDATIONS:

The views of patients should be taken into account at all stages in the development of patient information leaflets (PILs). Usable PILs, designed to meet the needs of patients and support the safe and appropriate use of medicines, must be the aim of all those involved in their preparation - not simply compliance with the law.

PILs should be made more usable by taking the opportunities presented by changes in the law to achieve the best possible content and presentation. To support this, new guidance on usability and on how to take account of the outcome of user consultations should be published for producers of PILs.

Sources of advice on writing information about health topics

This list is not exhaustive but provides useful pointers to sources of advice and guidance on writing about health topics that are relevant to the writing of PILs.

Plain English campaign   www.plainenglish.co.uk
This group offers advice and guidelines and can apply their quality 'Crystal Mark'.

RNIB - Royal National Institute of the Blind   www.rnib.org.uk
The RNIB offers advice on providing clear information in its See It Right Pack

Communication Research Institute of Australia   www.communication.org.au
The book, *Writing about medicines for people* by D Sless & R Wiseman, is available from this site. It draws on Australian experience of writing consumer medicines information. The website also lists other relevant Australian guidance.

Consumer Health Information Consortium (CHIC)   www.omni.ac.uk/CHIC/
This is an autonomous UK organisation run by and for people interested in the provision of high quality health information to the public. The website includes a list of resources on producing information, accessibility and quality assessment.

A practical guide which is only available in print is by Duman, M (2003) *Producing Patient Information* London, Kings Fund, ISBN 1857174704, £20, available from the Kings Fund Online bookshop.

*   *Two members of the Working Group, David Dickinson and Theo Raynor, had professional interests in companies which offered user testing services for PILs during the development of this guidance. All interests were declared to the MHRA in accordance with the published procedures and members did not take part in discussions on PILs for products in which they had declared an interest. The expertise of these members was, however, taken into account in the discussion of general principles for user testing and the development of the guidance in Annex 5. The Working Group also sought advice from Prof David Sless.*

References

1.   David Dickinson. Personal communication.

2.   Berry D C. Pyschol Health 1997

3.   European Commission. Excipients in the Labelling and Package Leaflet of Medicinal Products for Human Use. July 2003.

4.   European Commission. Guideline on the Readability of the Label and Package Leaflet of Medicinal Products for Human Use. September 1998.

5.   Sless D & Wiseman R Writing about medicines for people: Usability Guidelines for Consumer Medicine Information (2ndedition). Australian Government Publishing Service, Canberra, 1997.

6.   European Commission. Directive 2004/27/EC of the European Parliament and of the Council of 31 March 2004 amending Directive 2001/83/EC on the Community code relating to medicinal products for human use. March 2004.

4 COMMUNICATING RISK

SUMMARY

No effective medicine is completely risk free. Understanding the potential risks and benefits of a given course of treatment is fundamental to making an informed decision about it. Most medicine users will not have a clinician's technical, objective understanding about courses of treatment, but they can be helped to evaluate the possible advantages and disadvantages of treatment options much more effectively than has traditionally been the case. Accurate and effective communication about risk helps to build trust between patient and clinician and to counterbalance media 'scare stories' about medicines. This then gives the patient more informed control over his or her own medicine taking, and making a significant contribution to public health.

Whether or not a particular risk is acceptable is essentially a personal matter. Perception of, and attitudes to, risk are not simply the result of logical quantitative analysis but represent complex thought processes and are subject to many influences and biases, such as individual beliefs, values and level of trust in the information source [1][2][3].

PILs can be long and complex, and it is not always easy to extract the key messages. To address this the Group looked at the use of headline information, presented prominently at the beginning of a PIL, summarising carefully selected messages that are important to the safe and effective use of the medicine.

The information about possible side effects and other warnings which EU law requires the PIL to include can be alarming to medicine users. As well as better presentation of side effects information, the Group considered the inclusion of information about the potential benefit of the medicine, in order to provide balance and context when considering risk.

The law requires each PIL to provide information on all the side effects that have been identified for the medicine concerned, to present the information in a logical order and to include a description of the side effects, estimates of their frequency (or probability of occurring) and advice on any necessary actions. In practice there is a vast range of differing procedures and standards, indicating a need for more detailed guidance in this area.

No EU guidelines exist specifically for presentation of risk information in PILs, and current practice is highly variable. It will never be possible to cater for every aspect of every individual's perceptions about risk in a single PIL, but it should be possible to improve general standards of risk communication. Patient organisations and other experts have helped the Group to identify the main problems with risk communication in PILs, and we have developed flexible, practical guidance to the pharmaceutical industry which, together with user testing of all new PILs, will help to ensure that PILs meet medicine users' needs.

Key areas for guidance have been considered:

- putting the most important information first;

- including information on benefit;

- using the right words;

- using numbers appropriately to convey risk.

In addition to providing guidance on the optimal presentation of risk in PILs, the Working Group has considered the potential for developing a supplementary leaflet about the risks and benefits of medicines, which can be read in addition to PILs accompanying medicines and which provides general background information on the safe use of medicines.

4.1 RISK COMMUNICATION ABOUT MEDICINES – POTENTIAL IMPACT ON PUBLIC HEALTH

Patients naturally want to be involved in decisions relating to their health. Decisions such as whether to undertake a course of treatment, and which treatment to choose, can only be truly shared if the patient has a similar understanding of the possible advantages and disadvantages of each option as the clinician. Accurate and effective risk communication is therefore of great importance in establishing trust, reaching shared agreements and developing concordant clinical management plans.

In recent years, the safety of medicines has become the focus of intense media attention. High profile 'scare' stories about medicines have become frequent. The failure of such stories to communicate risk information in an accurate and balanced way can have serious public health consequences. One example has been the increased number of unwanted pregnancies after 'scares' about the contraceptive pill. Therefore, high quality risk communication has an important role for public health, both at an individual and population level.

4.1.1 Challenges in risk communication for medicines

Risk is the probability or likelihood of a negative or undesirable outcome. For medicines, a negative outcome usually means a harmful side effect. Risk communication in this context therefore provides understandable information on:

(a)   the harmful effect itself;

(b)   the probability of it occurring; and ideally

(c)   how to minimise this risk and what actions to take in the event of a problem.

The level of trust placed in the information source is also an important factor in determining the effectiveness of the information provided[24]. Trust in large organisations such as governments and pharmaceutical companies is far from universal, but transparency and a willingness to share uncertainties about information are likely to be helpful.

Patient information leaflets cannot possibly deal with every nuance of risk perception or cater for the needs of every patient. However, good quality risk communication is worth striving towards and should be achievable.

For patients to make informed choices about the use of medicines, they should also understand the probability and nature of the beneficial effects of the medicine, and consider possible benefit and harm side by side. Achieving this within a single document is far from straight-forward. Providing an accessible format and concise descriptions to convey drug side effects and their seriousness without being alarmist can be difficult. Likewise, great care is needed when providing statistical information to ensure that it presents risks in a clear and unbiased way.

4.2 RISK COMMUNICATION IN PATIENT INFORMATION LEAFLETS – CURRENT PRACTICE

The meeting with patients' organisations and the reports described in Chapter 3 indicate that one of the key problems with patient information leaflets is the way in which the inherent risks with a medicine are communicated. Particular concerns related to the lack of balanced information in relation to benefit and the lack of clarity or hierarchy in the way in which the side effects are set out. A major contributory factor may be the lack of specific guidance in this area.

4.2.1 Existing guidance on writing patient information leaflets

Little guidance on risk communication is available to those writing patient information leaflets and there are no formal EU guidelines. Some information on how to express side effects is included in the readability guideline which recommends that information about side effect incidence should be conveyed to the patient where these data are available. In addition, the guidance also recommends that very serious, typical undesirable effects should be mentioned first or specially highlighted, irrespective of their frequency. This applies in particular where there is an urgent need for the patient to take action. Another method of presenting this section of the leaflet, if frequency data are not available, is according to the seriousness of the side effects or the body system affected.

The measures to be taken to remedy or alleviate undesirable effects should be mentioned. If a patient needs to seek help urgently, the term "immediately" is recommended. For less urgent conditions, use of the phrase "as soon as possible" may be used. At the end of the side effects section, the patient should be invited to communicate any undesirable effect, especially if it is not mentioned in the leaflet, to a doctor or pharmacist.

Nevertheless, it is fair to say that, although the advice offered within this guidance document is helpful, it is far from comprehensive and is certainly not applied consistently across all patient information leaflets currently available.

4.3 IMPROVING THE COMMUNICATION OF RISK IN PATIENT INFORMATION LEAFLETS

In considering how best to improve the way in which risk is communicated in patient information, the Working Group undertook a number of fact finding exercises. A literature review was conducted to identify concepts associated with risk and risk expression and to bring members to a common understanding of the factors involved. Separately, expert advice was sought from members and external advisors, including patient group representatives.

A meeting with patient groups in July 2004 (see Chapter 3) helped to bring the users' perspective into the Group's thinking. At this meeting the MHRA also introduced the proposals set out below to improve risk communication in PILs by including key points as a summary at the start, giving information on the benefits of taking the medicines and guidance on presenting statistical information. The views of attendees on the proposals were generally positive and a number of constructive suggestions were made on how to improve the comprehensibility of the information, on important information that needed to be conveyed and proposals for how to achieve this. These were taken into account in finalising the Working Group's guidance.

4.4 REVIEW OF THE RELEVANT LITERATURE

4.4.1 General aspects of risk perception

Risk perception is a complex cognitive function and subject to many influences. Not only does it (usually) require some understanding of statistical probability, but is likely to be influenced by beliefs and values. Different personality types may also affect the way individuals approach the subject of risk. For example, some individuals might generally take a 'fatalistic' approach to risk (ie assume that it is futile to attempt to control risk), while others may prefer to manage risks actively (eg by rules and regulations, public consultation or individual risk assessment)[1,2].

4.4.2 Biases in thinking about risk

Common biases in thinking about risk have been identified in the literature. These include:

Awareness bias: whereby increased awareness of an issue (eg through media reports) can lead to an exaggerated perception of risk;

Optimistic bias: whereby individuals tend to rate their chances of avoiding mishap as 'better than average';

New risk bias: new risks generate more fear than risks that have been experienced for some time;

Catastrophic bias: risks that are perceived as catastrophic, eg those killing many people at once in one place, are feared more than those that are chronic, killing an equal or greater number of people but over time and in scattered locations.

4.4.3   Fright factors

Risks are generally more worrying[3] (and less acceptable) if perceived as:

- involuntary rather than voluntary;

- inequitably distributed (some benefit while others suffer the consequences);

- inescapable by taking personal precautions;

- arising from an unfamiliar or novel source;

- resulting from man-made, rather than natural sources;

- causing hidden and irreversible damage, eg through illness after many years of exposure;

- posing some particular danger to small children or pregnant women or, more generally, to future generations;

- threatening a form of death (or illness/injury) arousing particular dread;

- damaging to identifiable rather than anonymous victims;

- poorly understood by science;

- subject to contradictory statements from responsible sources (or, even worse, from the same source).

4.4.4   Sources of information and trust

Whether or not information on risk is heeded can be heavily influenced by the level of trust that is put in the source of the information. In general terms, information arising from large organisations, corporations, governments and their Agencies is trusted less than that from individual credible professionals, such as doctors or scientists[24].

4.4.5 Expression of risk from a regulatory perspective

At present, the main emphasis in expressing risk from a regulatory perspective (SPCs and PILs) is in terms of statistical probability and corresponding verbal descriptors - eg 'very rare' corresponds to 'up to 0.01% (less than 1 per 10,000)'.

Verbal Descriptor	EU assigned frequency*
Very common	> 10% (more than 1 per 10)
Common	>1% and <10% (less than 1 per 10 but more than 1 per 100)
Uncommon	0.1% to 1% (less than 1 per 100 but more than 1 per 1000)
Rare	0.01% to 0.1% (less than 1 per 1000 but more than 1 in 10,000)
Very rare	up to 0.01% (less than 1 per 10,000)

*Key: > more than   < less than

The available literature suggests that a statistical approach to describing risk is often met with satisfaction by the recipients. However, research into what individuals understand by terms such as 'very rare', 'common' etc[5][6], suggests that the current EU guidelines on verbal descriptors are not correctly matched with statistical probabilities. In general, it appears that the public equate the verbal descriptors (very rare, common etc) to risks that are substantially higher than those defined in regulatory documents. Perceiving very small risks is particularly problematic and a number of models have been proposed in the literature to help with this. One scale[7] is based on a different set of verbal descriptors (high, moderate, low, very low and minimal), but this too may not be in accord with people's actual interpretations. Other scales attempt to relate potentially hazardous events to familiar concepts such as:

- scales relating the size of various communities as risk comparators one/street/town etc[7];

- a scale using the risk of other events such as car accident, murder, lightning as comparators[8][9].

Meaningful interpretation, however, necessitates a reasonable familiarity with the comparator.

4.4.6 Other issues relating to statistical information

Other issues relating to effective expression of the statistical magnitude of risk have been discussed in the literature. The main points are summarised below:

- denominators: it is better to use the same denominator throughout when describing more than one risk[8];

- relative and absolute risk: it is helpful to express information on relative and absolute risks, so that the baseline risk and risk attributable to the medicine are clearly identified[10];

- framing: perceptions of statistical risk can be influenced by either positive or negative 'framing' (eg a 1/100 risk of adverse outcome is equivalent to a 99/100 chance of no harmful effect, but the perception of these two statements may be quite different)[8 11];

- use of diagrams (eg bar charts) and pictures can be helpful in describing statistical probabilities[8 12].

4.4.7 Format: word, number and pictures

There is no single format of risk description that caters optimally for every situation. Choice of words and style of language is clearly important in conveying qualitative and quantitative aspects of risk. In some situations, pictures and numbers can assist understanding.

4.5 MOVING TOWARDS BETTER RISK COMMUNICATION

The main areas considered by the Working Group are discussed below. In some areas an iterative approach was taken to developing and reviewing ideas. In this way, the Group was able to try out new concepts (with worked examples) to see how risk communication principles identified in the literature translated into PILs. In some cases, the concepts considered were not seen to be useful in PILs and were consequently not taken forward into the final guidance document.

4.5.1   General aspects of risk perception and risk individualisation

Trust and recognition

PILs are produced by the relevant MA holder and PILs frequently have the logo of the relevant pharmaceutical company. Whether or not an MHRA logo or 'seal of approval'/quality mark would influence patients' views on the validity or trustworthiness of the document is unclear. Much would depend on the public reputation and standing of the MHRA. This is one possible area for consideration in the context of the MHRA's proposals to increase public recognition of its role.

Transparency is an effective method of improving trust in many situations. Improved transparency over the sources of data and certainty/uncertainty of risk estimates presented in PILs might therefore be helpful in establishing trust. Whilst it would not be possible to reference every source of information in PILs, directing the reader to additional background information could be helpful in establishing trust, especially if the additional source would generally be regarded as being highly credible.

Attention to 'fright factors'

The literature suggests that a number of 'fright factors' (see section 4.4.3) might generally cause exaggerated concerns. Providing clear information on the true scale and nature of such risks in PILs is therefore important. The Working Group has considered a number of approaches which might be particularly valuable when referring to potential 'fright factors'. Such approaches include:

- use of analogies and alternative risk scales to represent rarity of risk;

- describing baseline risk and increased risk with the drug;

- provision of further information sources on these risks.

Individualising risks

Inevitably, PILs can only describe risks as they apply to the population as a whole. Patients might therefore benefit from some guidance in the PIL about factors that could modify particular risks, so that they can interpret the general information in a way that is relevant for each individual. The Group therefore supported the development of generic supplementary information on risks and benefits, which could contain a range of information regarding safe use of medicines, including general information about risk factors for side effects, and risk minimisation. This is further discussed below at section 4.5.5.

4.5.2   Access to the most important information for safe and effective use: headlines

The length and apparent complexity of PILs is likely to be a disincentive to read the document[13]. Although European and national legislation demand that PILs contain comprehensive clinical information, extra-statutory information is permitted and this provides an opportunity to improve the accessibility of key messages.

Headline information, presented prominently at the beginning of a PIL and summarising a few key messages for safe and effective use, is one option that has been considered in depth by the Working Group. Such 'headlines' could not attempt to summarise all the information in the PIL, but could include carefully selected messages that are important.

The Group took into account the development of "Drug Facts" established in the US for over the counter medicines, which alert patients to key safety messages about a particular medicine.

The Group looked at whether or not the use of such headlines needed to have a sound evidence base and considered the need for user testing on their content and impact on the patient reading the rest of the leaflet. Although there appears to be no published evidence to support this additional information within the PIL, the requirement placed on marketing authorisation holders to undertake consultations with target patient groups would provide evidence on individual PILs which will go some way to addressing this concern.

The proposals for headline information were also endorsed at the patient meeting in July 2004 and tested in practice during discussion of the Seroxat PIL by a focus group of representatives from SSRI patient interest and user groups (see section 3.1.3 for details).

Information that could be included in headlines

There is no set formula or list of issues that should be considered for headlines for every product but, for most products, it is likely that at least one or two key messages can be identified from the following:

- why the patient should take the product;

- the maximum dose or duration of treatment;

■ potential side effects/withdrawal reactions (symptoms to look out for, especially for common or serious side effects);

■ contraindications;

■ important drug interactions;

■ circumstances in which the drug should be stopped;

■ what to do if the medicine doesn't work; or

■ where to find further information.

As with other aspects of the PIL, it would be important to ensure that headlines do not appear alarmist or overly 'negative'. Careful wording and the use of a non-promotional statement of the licensed indication (for example, *"Your doctor has prescribed [PRODUCT] because it is a treatment for migraine headaches"*) at the start should help to ensure a balance is achieved.

It would also be important that headlines include a firm encouragement for the patient to read the rest of the leaflet. The following concluding headline was proposed. Inclusion of the date of latest revision may be helpful to long-term medicines users who would not otherwise realise that the PIL has changed since they last read it.

"Now read the rest of this leaflet. *It includes other important information on the safe and effective use of this medicine that might be especially important for you.* ***This leaflet was last updated on xx/xx/xx."***

How headlines might appear – an example

On the following page is an example of six headlines which the Group decided were possible for the anticonvulsant carbamazepine. As a general rule, it is unlikely that more than six headlines would be helpful.

Carbamazepine 200mg Tablets

Important things that you need to know:

■ Carbamazepine tablets are prescribed for different illnesses including epilepsy, manic-depression and neuralgia.

■ **Take carbamazepine regularly to get the maximum benefit.** You should not stop taking the medicine without talking to your doctor. Sometimes stopping the medicine can cause problems.

■ Carbamazepine can cause side effects, although most people do not have serious problems – see page 2 for details. If you have fever, sore throat, skin rashes or skin yellowing, mouth ulcers, bruising or bleeding, see your doctor immediately.

■ Some side effects may occur early in treatment. These often disappear after a few days as your body gets used to the drug (for example dizziness, drowsiness or clumsiness).

■ Taking other medicines, including other anti-epilepsy drugs, may sometimes cause problems. Check with your doctor or pharmacist before taking any other medicines.

■ If you are (or might become) pregnant while taking carbamazepine, it is important to talk to your doctor about this.

Now read the rest of this leaflet. It includes other important information on the safe and effective use of this medicine that might be especially important for you. **This leaflet was last updated on xx/xx/xx**

4.5.3 Striking a balance – conveying information on benefits as well as risks

A common criticism of PILs is that much of the advice and information relates to possible side effects and other warnings, and that this can appear frightening and might dissuade some patients from taking their medicines[14]. Clearly, a balance should be struck between providing information on all possible side effects (as is required in EU legislation) and being non-alarmist. To some extent the problem can be tackled by ensuring that information on side effects is presented optimally (see section 4.5.4), but a further option is to include 'positive' information in the PIL about the potential benefits of taking the medicine.

Currently, the section of the PIL entitled *"What is your medicine and how does it work"* includes information on the pharmacotherapeutic group to which the medicine belongs and the indications for which it is authorised. The inclusion of more information about the benefits of taking the medicine in this section would be extra-statutory, but consistent with current legislation. In addition, there is evidence from the literature that short factual statements on the benefits of medicines can help patients weigh up the risks and benefits of the medicine.[15.]

As with 'headline' information, there is no single formula for including benefit information that is likely to be appropriate for all medicines. Any additional information should be compatible with the Summary of Product Characteristics, useful to the patient and should not be promotional. The Group considered that some of the following issues could be covered in a few sentences (about 80 words or less):

- why it is important to treat the disease and what the likely clinical outcome would be if the disease remained untreated;

- whether the treatment is for short term or chronic use;

- whether the medicine is being used to treat the underlying disease (ie curative) or for control of symptoms. If the latter, which symptoms will be controlled and how long the effects will last;

- whether the effects will last after the medication is stopped;

- where the medicine is used to treat two or more discrete indications, all should be succinctly described as above;

- where to obtain more information on the condition.

It would seem likely that 'benefit' information would be most helpful for prescription medicines and, in particular, preventative or long-term treatments. On the following page is an example of how the expanded information might appear for an inhaled corticosteroid for the prevention of asthma. This concept has gained support from the Group and from a number of patient group representatives who attended the meeting at the MHRA in July 2004.

Without benefit information

PRODUCT contains beclometasone propionate which is one of a group of medicines called corticosteroids. These have an anti-inflammatory action and are used to treat asthma.

With benefit information

PRODUCT contains beclometasone propionate which is one of a group of medicines called corticosteroids, or "steroids". Corticosteroids prevent attacks of asthma by reducing swelling of the air passages and are sometimes called "preventers". You should take this medicine regularly every day even if your asthma is not troubling you. Using PRODUCT can help prevent severe asthma attacks which sometimes need hospital treatment and if left untreated could even be life-threatening.

This medicine should not be used to treat a sudden asthma attack; it will not help. You will need to use a different inhaler ("reliever") to deal with these attacks.

4.5.4 Better information about side effects

Many patients want to know about the risks attached to taking their medicine and whether symptoms that they experience might be a side effect. Crucially, all patients need to know what to do if they encounter serious problems.

Ideally, PILs should provide information on all the side effects that have been identified for a particular medicine. The information should be provided in a logical order and include a description of the side effects, estimates of their frequency (or probability of occurring) and advice on any necessary actions. However, although these principles are straightforward, examination of current PILs reveals a vast range of differing practice and standards and the need for more detailed guidance in this area. The sections below cover the main areas and principles that the Working Group decided to take forward with advice from the patient groups.

Putting the most important information first

It is likely that the order and style of presentation of side effects can greatly affect a patient's perception of the risks. The current guidelines[16] require a description of possible side effects consistent with the SPC and recommend that the most serious side effects requiring action are presented first. However, in many current PILs, side effects are simply put in order of body system, exactly as in the SPC.

There are many possible ways to categorise side effect information. The most important information for patients relates to those situations where they may need to take action, such as stopping the medicine or seeking medical help. Separating this type of information from less important issues and placing it first therefore seems logical. In some cases, early identification and prompt action could avert major consequences. Examples of side effects that would fall into this category are:

- gastrointestinal bleeding with non-steroidal anti-inflammatory medicines;

- angioedema/facial swelling with any medicine;

- tendon pain with fluoroquinolones;

- unexplained muscle pain with statins;

- painful swollen leg (possible deep venous thrombosis) with oral contraceptives.

Usually, the most serious side effects are also the rarest and in order to avoid unnecessary alarm, it would be important to include information on the frequency of such side effects wherever possible.

Using the right words

For all side effects, the description is critical to patients' understanding. Ideally, the description should convey an accurate impression of the side effect, including the symptoms that patients are likely to experience. For example, gastrointestinal bleeding would be recognised by the patient as either black or blood-stained vomiting or stools, often with abdominal pain.

Words should be carefully chosen not only to describe the side effect, but also to convey seriousness or severity. This is particularly important for conditions that are unfamiliar to most patients and might otherwise be misunderstood. For example, any description of rhabdomyolysis should not simply describe muscle breakdown, but should also mention the severity of symptoms and the possible serious complications.

Many side effects are dose-related. PILs should advise patients that higher doses, needed to achieve full benefit/efficacy in some patients, may be associated with an increased risk of side effects. A general warning statement may suffice in some circumstances, but care is needed to ensure that the warning is not alarmist to those who have been prescribed high doses. Specific statements relating to individual side effects may be appropriate if an important dose-relationship exists (eg muscle side effects with statins).

Glossary of lay terms

There are many factors to consider when describing side effects. Currently, descriptions of side effects are submitted by companies and assessed individually for each PIL, resulting in differing and inconsistent terminology. For patients, who may read about the same side effect described in two or more quite different ways, this inconsistency is likely to be unhelpful. Standardisation of side effect terminology would therefore seem desirable, and adoption of 'preferred lay terms' for specific side effects would also be helpful to industry and regulators. The Group has endorsed a proposal to develop a glossary of side effect terms, and a current draft of the first 56 terms is at Annex 8. It is envisaged that further terms will be added to the glossary.

Conveying risk with numbers

Conveying the concept of small risks has been discussed in section 4.4.5 and options include reference to scales such as those discussed there. All these scales suffer a limitation however in that meaningful interpretation necessitates a reasonable familiarity with the comparator, and an individual's perception of the risk of a comparator event may be heavily influenced by their own experiences. For example, someone who has witnessed or been involved in a car accident might have a completely different perception of this risk compared to someone who has not. Thus, although conceptually attractive, the use of analogies to convey the magnitude of risk is itself prone to bias and has not been taken forward into guidelines.

The Working Group and patient groups have considered the suitability of a variety of approaches to expressing statistical risk in PILs. A number of key principles have been identified from worked examples.

i.   *Quantifying risk:* use of absolute numbers eg 1 in 10,000 patients. If possible, baseline risk and absolute excess risks should be presented.

ii. *Verbal descriptors of risk* (eg 'very rare') should only be used if accompanied by the equivalent statistical information. For example: "Very rarely (fewer than 1 in 10,000 patients treated)...".

iii. *Conveying uncertainty around risk estimates:* imprecision of point estimates should be conveyed using terms such as 'approximately'/'about'/'around' when referring to estimates for major safety issues (for example *"about 5 extra cancers for every 1000 patients treated"*). The Group considered an alternative approach of including a range of values (for example *"between 3-7 extra cancers for every 1000 patients treated"*), but worked examples of PILs have shown this can lead to cumbersome statistics, and it is not clear that showing such ranges of risk would improve patient understanding, or modify perceptions.

iv. *Frequency ranges:* to simplify descriptions, it is preferable to use only the upper bound for each range. For example, use *'fewer than 1 in every 1,000'* rather than 'between 1 in 10,000 and 1 in 1,000'. Worked examples have shown that this approach lessens the burden of statistical information in PILs and may therefore improve readability.

v. *Duration of risk:* it is important to state the duration over which the excess risk applies if this is known. For example, the risk of serious blood disorders with the antipsychotic medicine clozapine is known to differ during the first 18 weeks versus weeks 19-52, and weeks 53 and above. Another example is the excess of risk of cancer associated with hormone replacement therapy (HRT) that can be stated in relation to the number of years of treatment. Similarly, if it is known that specific side effects may occur shortly after starting the drug and are likely to be transient, this information is helpful to include in the PIL.

vi. *Frequency estimates based on spontaneous adverse drug reaction (ADR) data:* reporting rates are likely to be an underestimate of true incidence or risk. This should be stated in the PIL when referring to data based only on spontaneous ADR data.

vii. *Constant denominators:* in some cases, it may be helpful to express the risk of adverse reactions using a 'constant denominator', for instance when expressing small differences in risk. Worked examples based on existing PILs have suggested that constant denominators might appear confusing when comparing greatly differing risks; for example, comparing a risk of 1 in 100 versus 1 in 10,000 would be represented as *100 in 10,000 versus 1 in 10,000.* Consultation with patient groups suggested the use of constant denominators might occasionally be appropriate; however, user testing will be key to ensuring that this concept is understandable.

Constant numerator (1)	Constant denominator (10,000)
1 in 10,000	1 in 10,000
1 in 1,000	10 in 10,000
1 in 100	100 in 10,000

Risk using constant numerators and constant denominators

A number of concepts have been considered to be inappropriate to take forward for general guidance. Some of these are discussed below.

- *NNT/NNH.* Numbers needed to treat or harm[17][18] are calculated as the reciprocal of absolute reduction or increase in risk. Such calculations are most accurately obtained from clinical trial data, and the most useful comparisons are with placebo. However, robust, placebo-controlled clinical trial data regarding important risks are not always available. A further disadvantage of NNT/NNHs is that they are usually dependent upon duration of treatment. This means that an NNT based on a clinical trial of two years duration is only relevant for patients who take the medicine for this period of time. As it is not routinely possible to calculate NNTs in PILs, and as the calculations may be subject to misinterpretation, this concept has not been taken forward into guidelines.

- *Positive framing and negative framing.* This concept was also informally tested in worked examples and found to be too cumbersome and lengthy for PILs. In addition to these concerns, patient groups did not find the concept helpful and were concerned that 'positive framing' might resemble a marketing ploy rather than a genuine attempt to provide balanced information. An example of positive and negative framing is shown below.

> The following side effects may affect fewer than 1 in 10,000 people. This means that at least 9,999 out of 10,000 people are not expected to experience one of these side effects....

- *Use of diagrams:* diagrams can be helpful but constraints on size means that these could only rarely be used in PILs and no formal guidance on their presentation has therefore been taken forward.

4.5.5   Supplementary information – a leaflet about risks and benefits

PILs provide comprehensive information that is specific for one medicine. Understanding this information and putting it to best use may require at least a rudimentary prior understanding about medicines and their side effects, and some patients may lack this understanding. In order to address this, the following general leaflet on risks and benefits of medicines was developed by the Working Group.

Benefits and side effects of medicines – some questions and answers

What is this leaflet about?

This leaflet aims to answer some questions you may have about taking medicines and the risk of side effects. You will find more information about your particular medicine in **the patient information** leaflet provided with your medicine.

If you have received a medicine but no leaflet, please ask your pharmacist to get one for you.

Need further advice?

If you need further advice about medicines remember you can ask your doctor or pharmacist or call NHS Direct & NHS Wales/Galw Iechyd Cymru on 0845 46 47 (text phone 0845 606 46 47) or NHS 24 (Scotland) on 08454 24 24 (textphone 18001 08454 24 24).

---

1. How do medicines work?

The medicine you are taking may:

- **cure your condition** – for example an antibiotic, which is used to treat an infection;
- **control your condition** – for example a medicine to lower your blood pressure;
- **treat the symptoms of your condition** – for example a painkiller to take for toothache;
- **prevent you from becoming unwell** – for example a vaccination against disease.

2. Will my medicine cause side effects?

- The expected benefit of your medicine will usually be greater than the risk of suffering any harmful side effects.
- Most people take medicines without suffering any side effects.
- However, all medicines can cause problems. Your patient information leaflet will list all the known side effects linked to your medicine.

Important: most people take medicines without suffering any side effects.

3. What is meant by a "common" or "rare" side effect?

The chance (the risk) of having a side effect can be described using words or figures or both. This is how risk may be described in your patient information leaflet:

- **Very common** means that more than 1 in 10 people taking the medicine are likely to have the side effect.
- **Common** means that between 1 in 10 and 1 in 100 people are affected.
- **Uncommon** means that between 1 in 100 and 1 in 1,000 people are affected.
- **Rare** means that between 1 in 1,000 and 1 in 10,000 people are affected.
- **Very rare** means that fewer than 1 in 10,000 people are affected.

Remember, if a side effect has a risk of 1 in 10,000, then 9,999 out of every 10,000 people taking the medicine are not expected to experience that side effect.

4. Does a high dose increase the risk of side effects?

In general, a high dose of a medicine is more likely to cause side effects. However, high doses are sometimes needed to ensure maximum benefit.

To get the maximum benefit from your medicine you need to take the recommended dose for you.

- For medicines you have bought yourself, the dose is written on the carton or container label and in the patient information leaflet.
- For medicines that have been prescribed by your doctor, the dose will be on the pharmacy label. The doctor will have prescribed a dose for you that takes into account your age, weight, how ill you are and any other medicines you may be taking. Only change your dose if you have discussed it with your doctor first.
- With some medicines, you will start on a low dose that will gradually be increased over a period of weeks (or months). With other medicines you will stay on the same dose throughout your course of treatment.
- Sometimes, when you need to stop taking a medicine, your doctor will gradually reduce the dose to avoid unpleasant withdrawal effects. You should not increase or decrease the dose prescribed by your doctor unless you have discussed it with him/her first.

Important: check the patient information leaflet and speak to your doctor or pharmacist if you feel unwell after your dose has been increased.

5. How can I reduce the risk of side effects?

- Take your medicine as your doctor or pharmacist has advised you.
- Be careful about mixing medicines. Some medicines should not be taken together. Before taking a new medicine, it is important to tell your doctor or pharmacist about any other medicines you are already taking, including herbal remedies or any non-prescription medicines you may have bought for yourself in a pharmacy or supermarket.
- Understand about "risk factors". Sometimes risk factors increase the chance of your medicine causing side effects. These factors will vary depending on what medicine you are taking. For example, you may be able to lower your risk of side effects by not drinking alcohol or not eating certain foods during your course of treatment. Your patient information leaflet will tell you about any known risk and what you can do to reduce the chance of side effects.

6. Do side effects always come on straight away?

- It depends on the medicine and the person.
- Some side effects can happen immediately – for example an allergic reaction. Others might not start for several days or weeks – for example skin rashes – or even longer – for example stomach problems with some painkillers.
- In general, side effects are most likely when you start a new medicine or after your dose has been increased.
- Quite often, mild side effects will go away as your body adjusts to the new medicine or dose.

7. What should I do if I feel unwell after taking my medicine?

- Check your patient information leaflet: it may contain all the advice you need.
- If in doubt, speak to your doctor, nurse or pharmacist or call NHS Direct, NHS Direct Wales/Galw Iechyd Cymru or NHS 24 on the numbers given at the beginning of this leaflet.
- For worrying or serious effects you may have to stop taking the medicine, or need other treatment.
- For less serious side effects, you may be advised to continue with your medicine, or change the dose.
- You or your health adviser can report suspected side effects to the drug safety watchdog (MHRA). Telephone 020 7084 2000 to find out more.

8. Will my medicine affect my lifestyle?

- Although most medicines will not affect your lifestyle, some can. Examples are:
- Some medicines may affect your vision or co-ordination or make you sleepy. This may affect your ability to drive, ride a bicycle or perform skilled tasks safely.
- Some medicines may affect your sex drive.
- You may need to stop drinking alcohol or eating certain foods while taking some medicines.

Important: your patient information leaflet will tell you about any lifestyle issues and advise you about things you should avoid.

51

Patient groups were consulted in developing draft proposals for the leaflet about risks and benefits. The leaflet was also pilot tested at the MHRA. Annex 9 provides the protocol and results of the pilot testing.

The Group advised that this leaflet could be presented in a variety of different formats. Options include paper leaflets for doctors' surgeries or pharmacies, or electronic information for websites (eg MHRA and NHS Direct Online). Electronic formats could also be made available for health care professionals (eg in the National Electronic Library for Health), or for patients (eg 'My HealthSpace' – a secure place on the internet for patients to store information relevant to them).

4.6   CONCLUSION

There are no EU guidelines specifically dedicated to best practice in risk communication, and other existing guidelines to aid with the preparation of PILs contain relatively little advice on this subject. As a result, current practice in risk communication is highly variable and the outcome is often poor. There is scope within the current legal framework on PILs to develop risk communication guidelines and the future changes to the law will give further opportunities to assist with better risk expression in the leaflet. A number of options for consideration have been identified or derived from the literature. Discussion with patient representatives has highlighted a number of concerns which could be addressed in guidance. Selection and prioritisation of key principles that can be practically implemented in PILs were the first stages considered in the development of new guidance. The guidelines which have been developed can be found at Annex 10.

It is likely that the current variable standards of PILs in the UK are mirrored in other EU Member States, and the new guidance may therefore be of benefit in other countries. Once successfully launched in the UK, it should be possible to offer new approaches and principles for consideration within the EU.

Even with this guidance the Group recognises that it will only be when the final patient information leaflet is tested with patient groups that the full impact of the principles will be realised. The guidelines are living documents and as new evidence emerges from, for example user testing, the principles will be updated to reflect this knowledge.

RECOMMENDATIONS

The guidelines on risk communication included in this report should be the subject of wide consultation. In particular, views should be sought on the concepts of improved order and information on side effects, headline information targeting key messages, and short statements on benefits.

To promote consistency and clarity in the writing of PILs, a glossary of lay terms for describing side effects should be developed, tested and enlarged over time.

References

1. Eisner, Richard J. Communication and interpretation of risk. British Medical Bulletin 1998; 54 (No 4): 779-790.

2. Gray G M & Ropeik D P. Dealing with the Dangers of Fear: The Role of Risk Communication. Health Affairs 2002; 21 (No 6): 106-116.

3. Department of Health. Communicating about Risks to Public Health – Pointers to Good Practice. 1997.

4. Breakwell G M. Risk Communication: factors affecting impact. British Medical Bulletin 2000: 56 (No1) 110-120.

5. Reagan R T, Mosteller F & Youtz C. Quantitative meanings of verbal probability expressions. Journal of Applied Psychology 1989; 74: 433-442

6. Berry D C, Raynor D K & Knapp P. Communicating risk of medication side effects: an empirical evaluation of EU recommended terminology. Psychology, Health & Medicine 2003; 8 (No 3); 451-263.

7. Calman K C & Royston G H D. Risk, Language and Dialect. BMJ 1997; 315: 939-942

8. Paling J. Strategies to help patients understand risks. BMJ 2003; 237: 745-748

9. Paling J & Paling S. Up to your Armpits in Alligators. Florida; John Paling and Co Ltd 1996.

10. Stewart FH, Shields W C & Hwang A C. Presenting health risks honestly: mifepristone, a case in point. Contraception 2004; 69: 177-178.

11. Buetow S, Cantrill J & Sibbald B. Risk Communication in the Patient-Health Professional Relationship. Health Care Analysis 1998; 6: 261-270

12. Schapira M M, Nattinger AB & McHorney C A. Frequency or probability? A qualitative Study of Risk Communication Formats Used in Health Care. Medical Decision Making 2001; Nov-Dec: 459-467

13. Knapp P & Raynor D K. A telephone survey of patients' use of medicines information leaflets. PJ 1999; 263: R40-41

14. Berry D C, Michas I C & Bersellini. Communicating information about medication side effects: effects on satisfaction, perceived risk to health and intention to comply. Psychology & Health 2002; 17: 247-267.

15. Vander Stichele R H, Van Dierendonck A, De Vooght G, Reynvoet B & Lammertyn J. Impact of Benefit Messages in Patient Package Inserts on Subjective Drug Perception. Drug Information Journal 2002; 26: 201-208.

16. European Commission. Guideline on the Readability of the Label and Package Leaflet of Medicinal Products for Human Use. September 1998.

17. Cook D & Sackett D. The number needed to treat: a clinically useful measure of treatment effect. BMJ 1995; 310:452-454.

18. Holden W I, Juhaeri J & Dai W. Benefit-risk analysis: examples using quantitative methods. Pharmacoepidemiology and Drug Safety 2003; 12: 693-697

5 MEETING THE NEEDS OF SPECIAL GROUPS OF PATIENTS

SUMMARY

For many medicine users, a well written, clearly designed PIL has the potential to be an important source of information, but not everyone finds it easy to access and use information in this way. For example some visually impaired people, some who have a first language other than English, people with poor basic skills in language, literacy and numeracy and some people with learning difficulties or physical difficulties may have problems. Children who take medicines and their parents, and carers who help others take medicines, may also have information needs for which the standard PIL does not cater.

The Group has reviewed the needs of some of these groups of people and has identified a number of areas of potential to increase the utility of the PIL and the information it contains. These include making the PIL available in other formats and signposting the availability of information from other sources. The Working Group will continue to look at ways of meeting the needs of diverse groups within the population.

5.1 INTRODUCTION

Recognising the importance of the information in the PIL in promoting safe use of medicines, the Group was keen to ensure that as many people as possible had access to this information. The Group was also mindful of other health and educational initiatives that can assist in the provision of information about medicines to consumers. They recognised that the ability to use the information in the PIL was linked to health literacy, and that measures to promote health literacy could therefore help to ensure that everyone could get the most out of the PIL. The Group's aim is that improvements to the PIL should not simply serve to increase the knowledge and health of only some people, and so inadvertently increasing health inequalities. Consultation with patient organisations and other relevant groups is a priority for the Group in taking forward this work.

5.2 HEALTH LITERACY AND WIDER GOVERNMENT INITIATIVES

Health literacy has been defined as "the degree to which individuals have the capacity to obtain, process and understand basic health information and services needed to make appropriate health decisions"[1]. As a component of this, medication literacy would refer to the range of skills needed to access, understand and act on medicines information. The concept is a useful tool in identifying problems in communicating health information and enabling people to use that information to make health decisions.

The Department of Health (DH) in its report *Choosing Health: making healthier choices easier*[2] highlighted the need to 'tailor information and advice to meet people's needs and support staff to communicate complex health information to different groups in the population' and 'provide practical support for people who lack basic skills to help them use health information, including signposting them to extra support'.

Another DH report, *Management of Medicines*[3], also identified as a priority those patients for whom English was not their first language and/or whose health literacy is low.

The ideas in *Choosing Health* were carried forward in *Better information, better choices, better health: putting information at the centre of health*[4]. This also fulfilled one of the six key priorities of *Building on the best: choice, responsiveness and equity in the NHS*[5], to make "the right information available at the right time with the support they need to use it".

The *Better information* strategy seeks to deliver by 2008 the aim that 'disadvantaged groups have access to and use information as much as other groups'. The report suggests effective signposting as a way of tackling inequalities in accessing information and seeks to use a policy of empowerment as a way of enabling people to access and use health information. Primary Care Trusts are required to work in partnership with other organisations to ensure people have access to a broad range of information which is sensitive to their needs. Equally, pharmacies will be expected to take part pro-actively and contribute to national and local campaigns.

A number of projects are being set up in partnership with internal and external stakeholders to deliver aspects of the strategy as follows:

- a health search engine to help healthcare staff and the public sift and judge information;

- a Patient Information Bank for NHS Trusts to use to print consistent information for individuals about their care and treatment;

- an accreditation scheme and quality marks to help people judge the quality of the information they use;

- power questions for people to ask professionals at consultations;

- an 'information prescription' to signpost people to further sources of information;

- a continuing focus on 'copying letters to patients';

- support in the community for people to access and use information, including 'navigators' to access information easily in ways people trust;

- NHS Direct Interactive on digital TV to provide accredited information to people's homes;

- a code of practice on communications for professionals;

- a national information forum as a single route to prioritise and commission information nationally.

It is important to address the social and cultural obstacles to health literacy[6 7] so that people who may have experienced low self esteem and/or alienation can feel confident and enabled in making informed decisions on the safe use of medicines. Links to other initiatives such as SureStart, Skilled for Health, Healthy Cities and the Social Exclusion Unit (SEU) initiatives on improving services for disadvantaged adults could help to promote the social and cultural changes required to improve health literacy.

5.3 PATIENTS WITH POOR BASIC SKILLS

The Basic Skills Agency for England and Wales defines basic skills as "the ability to read, write and speak in English/Welsh and to use mathematics at a level necessary to function at work and society in general"[8].

Links between poor basic skills and self reported poor health and between low educational achievement and poor health are well documented[9 10]. The Department for Education and Skills (DfES) survey of literacy, numeracy and Information and Communications Technology (ICT) skills[11] found that nearly half of all adults aged 16-65 were classified at entry level three or below in at least one of the two skills (literacy and numeracy), ie the skill level expected of 11 year olds. Those in poor health were particularly likely to lack basic skills[11].

People with limited reading ability will face problems reading the statutory patient information leaflet. They are also at a higher risk of not getting the treatment needed because of a failure to understand the information they receive. A significant proportion of people of all ages also have low numeracy skills and this may mean that they are unable to understand the dosage instructions. The US Center for Health Care Strategies cites research which showed that hospital patients with poor health literacy skills were five times more likely to misinterpret their prescriptions than those with adequate skills[12].

A clearly written PIL in plain English, taking into account the presentation issues discussed elsewhere in this report, will increase the number of people who can access the information contained in the PIL. This, together with the DfES and other national education department programmes to improve basic skills, should mean that more people can read and understand the PIL. Using the PIL to signpost other sources of information, and provision of a universal PIL helpline, would also increase the utility of the PIL and assist in reducing inequalities.

5.4 PATIENTS WITH SIGHT LOSS

Patient information leaflets are provided in a standard text format. As a result, people with sight loss have to rely on either remembering spoken information or asking a family member or carer to read medical information to them. The alternative is not having the information at all. This kind of information provision can result in several negative outcomes that disadvantage people with sight loss:

- the loss of privacy associated with having someone else read information about personal medical care and treatment;

- not being fully informed about treatments;

- being less able to participate in decisions about treatments;

- gaining less benefit from the medicines prescribed.

The problems faced by people with sight loss in accessing information about their medicines are similar to those they face in other aspects of their life. Many people with some degree of sight loss can read large and clear print so well-designed leaflets can help some of this group, although there are obvious size and space restrictions on PILs in medicine packs. Other sources of information include large print formats, audio tapes, information via touch-tone telephones and talking web pages. Braille is one option for information provision, although it is recognised that very few patients are competent with Braille. Braille tends to be used by those who have had blindness since birth whereas for most of the 1.7 million people with sight loss in the UK, sight loss started in later life. The extent to which alternative formats are made available is dependent on the awareness and commitment of providers, with large differences between providers likely.

People with sight loss are also likely to have varying preferences for information formats, and these preferences might be patterned by factors such as age and technological confidence. The language spoken by the person with sight loss is also important in determining access to information, such that the provision of audio-taped information only in English will exclude most of those whose first language is not English.

Alternative methods of information provision were identified and include:

■ leaflets available in Braille or large print;

■ an audio version made available through CD or tape;

■ leaflets able to be accessed via the web;

■ digital television;

■ telephone helplines and automated voice systems.

There would need to be a means of alerting patients to the availability of these services.

5.5 PATIENTS WHOSE FIRST LANGUAGE IS NOT ENGLISH

Research has shown that patients whose first language is not English may often also have low levels of health literacy. The Skills for Life survey[11] showed that among people whose first language was not English, 46% were entry level 3 or below for literacy and 69% were entry level 3 or below for numeracy.

In terms of enabling strategies, the DfES has set up an ESOL (English for Speakers of Other Languages) programme to try to overcome problems with functional literacy. The social and cultural obstacles to gaining full health literacy also need to be addressed in an appropriate way, in order that these groups of people can also make informed decisions about their health and the safe use of medicines[13].

The PIL must be written in the official language of the member state (for the UK this is English). For those who have limited command of English, helpful options are to use plain English for the PIL and to provide it in additional languages. Any translated leaflets should be based on the UK version and the quality of translation checked. Simple translation is not enough; cultural differences would also need to be considered. Telephone translation services could also be made available. Digital television could be used as a means of supporting patients who do not speak English as a first language.

Pictorial representations of the information were considered but were felt to be subject to limitations because they could not be comprehensive and had to be accompanied by verbal information to be understood. There were also culturally sensitive issues that would need to be taken into account.

Key solutions identified include:

- provision of leaflets in other languages available from the company in written or web-based format;

- telephone helplines;

- the use of translator services.

There would need to be a means of directing patients to these services.

5.6 MEDICINES FOR CHILDREN AND YOUNG PEOPLE

Children and young people need information about their medicines just as adult patients do. They also need education to support their progressive adoption of responsibility for medicine use.

Patient information leaflets are not tested on children and can be difficult for them to use. However, there is little evidence available on this. For chronic conditions, the leaflet should provide information with the aim of helping young people progressively to learn to manage their own condition. At all ages young people may be worried about medicine-taking so information about the consequences of not taking the medicine can be important.

Young children should generally have the information necessary communicated to them by parents or other carers and, consequently, the information should be aimed at adults in a sufficiently detailed form to enable a simple explanation of the key points to be communicated to the young child.

Young people from around the age of 14 can consider the consequences of health-related action, and by 15 they can make independent decisions about their medicine taking. Information targeted for these groups needs to take account of the lifestyle of the age group concerned and their likely questions.

There will be certain medicines available over the counter which older children and teenagers may purchase and use without adult supervision. Information accompanying these products should consider and take into account their likely needs and concerns.

The British National Formulary for Children will be a useful data source when available.

5.7 PROVISION OF INFORMATION TO CARERS

Carers include both formal carers, such as care staff, and informal carers such as family and friends. Any of the groups previously considered could include people with caring responsibilities.

A carer would probably not have participated in the consultation where a medicine was prescribed. Important information provided at the consultation when the medicine was prescribed and when it was dispensed may not have been shared with the carer who may also not have received the PIL.

Carers may need training on administration techniques. Particular issues identified were "off label" use where the PIL may not cover the pertinent information, what to do if the patient refuses the medication and how to dispose of surplus medicines.

Many of the information needs of carers, such as for information on when and how to take the product, are similar to those of other medicine users. It was recognised that many of the additional issues raised were outside the power of the Group to resolve but the use of a telephone helpline could address some of the concerns.

5.8 DEVELOPMENT OF OPTIONS TO ADDRESS SPECIAL NEEDS

It was clear to the Group that their work in improving the quality of PILs so that they are written in language that is generally accessible and are well designed will maximise the number of people able to use the PIL. The guidance developed by the Group to promote the usability of the PIL is discussed in Chapter 3. The Group also identified specific measures that could be taken by the pharmaceutical industry to promote access to the information in the PIL and other measures that would help to ensure that people were aware of how they could access information about their medicines. Several other measures identified link into wider initiatives to promote health literacy and access to information about health choices.

Legal requirements

The review of medicines legislation to be implemented from October 2005 includes the following provision:

"The MAH shall ensure that the package information leaflet is made available on request from patients' organisation in formats appropriate for the blind and partially sighted." [14]

The Group has advised on guidance on how this provision should be implemented.

Voluntary measures

For other groups, the reviews of the various individual areas where people have special needs were brought together in order to identify common themes for further work.

Possible options to improve the accessibility of information have been developed into a portfolio of "information keys" for pharmaceutical companies. Companies are encouraged to consider the indications for the particular medicine and the likely target populations who would be the main users of their products. They could then use the keys to help identify additional measures which would promote the dissemination of information on safe use of their products to ensure that vulnerable groups can have access to it.

The portfolio which has been developed by the Group for consultation forms part of the guideline on usability of the leaflet at Annex 6. This has been designed to help companies respond to the legal requirement as well as taking other voluntary measures, and covers the following options.

- **Provision of leaflets in other formats.** These include large print, audiotape or CD, Braille and electronic versions for use with computer-based access technology.

- **How to make alternative formats available.** Advice includes how to signpost this in the leaflet and work with pharmacists and other health professionals

- **Translation of leaflets into other languages.**

- **Use of information mediators.** These may include support helplines and translation services.

- **Expert sources of advice.** These provide quality standards for accessible materials applicable to particular groups.

The PIL can also serve as a pointer to other sources of information and support for patients, including the vulnerable groups discussed above. The portfolio advises on signposting in the PIL to where patients can obtain further information. This can include links to patient organisations or health portals. Other modalities to facilitate access to information that may be provided by industry are also discussed. These can include additional non-promotional materials such as booklets, simplified leaflets, magazines, videos and websites.

Written information at the time of the consultation can be helpful to patients and support communication between patients and health care professionals. However, the PIL is not usually available at this time. The Group recognised that measures to increase the availability of the PIL by online means would facilitate its use as a support tool and also make it possible to access the current version of a PIL. This could be useful to both patients and people who dispense medicines.

The Group recognised that this was the start of a process and that wide consultation would be required on these proposals, particularly with patient organisations experienced in providing information in formats to meet patients' needs. There were also other disadvantaged groups whose needs had still to be considered.

RECOMMENDATIONS:

There should be more focus on providing information for patients who have difficulty in accessing the information in the usual PIL, or who have particular needs such as those arising from sight loss or poor basic skills.

The information needs of children, young people and carers should receive particular attention.

References

1. United States Department of Health and Human Service Office of Disease Prevention and Health Promotion. Healthy People 2010. 2004. http://www.healthypeople.gov/default.htm

2. Department of Health. Choosing Health: Making Healthier Choices Easier. CM 6374. TSO London 2004.

3. Department of Health. Management of Medicines: A resource to support implementation of the wider aspects of medicines management for the National Service Frameworks for Diabetes, Renal services and Long-Term Conditions. London 2004.

4. Department of Health. Better information, better choices, better health: putting information at the centre of health. London 2004.

5. Department of Health. Building on the best. London 2004.

6. Nutbeam D. Health Literacy as a public health goal: a challenge for contemporary health education and communication strategies into the 21st century. Health Promotion International, 15: 3: 259- 267.

7. Zarcadoolas C, Pleasant A, & Greer D S. Understanding Health Literacy: an expanded model. Health Promotion International, (Advanced access published 23 March 2005)

8. Basic Skills Agency. Definition of Basic Skills. www.basic-skills.co.uk.

9. Bynner J & Parsons S. It Doesn't Get Any Better. Basic Skills Agency, London 1977.

10. Acheson, Sir Donald. Report of the Independent Inquiry into Inequalities in Health. Chairman Sir Donald Acheson. TSO London 1998.

11. Williams J, Clemens S, Oleinkova K, & Tarvin K. The Skills for Life Survey: A national needs & impact survey of literacy, numeracy and ICT skills. DfES Research Brief RB490. TSO London 2003.

12. CHCS Centre for Health Care Strategies Inc. Health Literacy and Understanding Medical Information. Fact Sheet 4 of 9. Undated. http://www.chcs.org

13. Lawton J, Ahmad N, Hallowell N, Hanna L &Douglas M. Perceptions and experiences of taking oral hypoglycaemic agents among people of Pakistani and Indian origin: qualitative study. BMJ 2005; 330: 1247.

14. European Commission. Title V of Council Directive 2001/83/EC C (as amended) Article 56

6 DELIVERING PROGRESS IN IMPROVING PATIENT INFORMATION LEAFLETS

SUMMARY

Since the Working Group was established, significant progress has been achieved. The work covers the four main themes which address the key features of the remit for the Group. This chapter sets out future plans to take forward the achievements presented in earlier chapters.

- Engaging with other EU member states

- Taking forward the guidance on risk communication, usability and user testing and auditing the impact of the guidance

- Need for further research

- Publicity about the availability of PILs

6.1 PROGRESS TO DATE

6.1.1 Legislative changes

A statutory instrument was laid in Parliament in December 2004 to implement the legislative changes to patient information leaflets in the UK from 1 July 2005.

6.1.2 User testing guidance

Guidance for the pharmaceutical industry has been developed. This provides advice on how to meet their new legal obligation on ensuring that patient information leaflets reflect the results of consultation with target patient groups. The discussions on this are in Chapter 3 and the full guidance is appended in Annex 5.

6.1.3 Usability guidance

Guidance on usability was developed by the Working Group and considers in detail the factors which should be addressed when designing and setting out the information required in the patient leaflet. This is fully discussed in Chapter 3 and the guidance is available at Annex 6.

6.1.4   Guidance on risk communication and related documents

Poor risk communication in patient information has been a major area of concern. This has been an important focus for the Working Group which developed a range of guidance about better communication of risk to assist those writing patient information. This is discussed in Chapter 4 and copies of the guidance and other documents produced are available at Annexes 8, 9, and 10.

This package of guidance is the subject of a consultation with stakeholders, including health care professionals, patients and industry, to bring together views on how this can best be introduced to realise benefits to patients.

6.1.5   Development of information keys

The fourth strand of work related to a review of issues about access to information for disadvantaged patients. As part of the usability guidance, the Group has produced advice for industry on information keys. This looks particularly at measures to meet the information needs of patients with sight loss, patients whose first language may not be English, patients with poor basic skills, and children and carers. The guidance is available at Annex 6.

6.1.6   Case work examples

The Working Group provided advice on practical improvements to specific leaflets which resulted in improved PILs that addressed the specific needs of patients and safety issues:

■ an antidepressant (including recommendations from a patient focus group);

■ a paediatric analgesic preparation for a new patient population;

■ a cholesterol-reducing medicine available over the counter for the first time;

■ an oral product for acne with special safety issues.

6.2 FUTURE WORK

6.2.1 Engaging with other EU member states

Earlier parts of this report have explained how patient information leaflets are regulated by European legislation and there are harmonised procedures for the review of PILs across Europe for some products. The MHRA has been working with other European regulatory authorities to promote a common interpretation of the new legislation, to learn from the experience of other member states and to ensure that the principles adopted in UK guidance are also recognised in developing European guidelines. Work is in progress in the following areas:

- **Revision of the European readability guideline.** The UK is leading this jointly with the European Medicines Agency and will promote incorporation of the principles outlined in the usability guideline described in Section 3.3 and the principles for risk communication set out in the guideline described in Chapter 4.

- **Development of guidance on user testing.** The UK experience of early implementation of this new European legislative provision and the UK guidance developed by the Group will provide a helpful framework for the development of European guidance on how the requirement for "consultation with target patient groups" will be implemented across Europe.

6.2.2 Need for further research

The requirement for user testing introduced in the UK from July 2005 will make testing compulsory for new PILs, using the principles outlined in the guidance accompanying this report. This will provide a valuable test of the ability of the new guidance to ensure that patients are able to identify and understand the key information they need for safe use of these products.

To promote the benefits to be obtained from user testing of PILs, the MHRA proposes to commission user testing of model PILs for ten important medicines. These will be chosen from those with wide usage, specific safety concerns or an especially vulnerable target population.

Companies marketing products containing these active ingredients will be asked to amend their PILs to reflect the good practice identified in testing. This information will also be made available publicly and to other companies wishing to incorporate the principles into their PILs. This project should be part of a wider initiative to develop prototypes and further guidance on designing and writing PILs so that patients can find and use the information they need for safe use of their medicines.

The risk communication guideline discussed in Chapter 4 provides guidance on conveying information about the benefits of taking the medicine. The Group considered that there was a need for further research to determine what specific types of information patients find helpful. Potential areas include how statistical information should be given where available, and when information about risks of not taking medicines is helpful and how this should be conveyed.

The Group also considered that more research would be helpful on tailoring information to groups and individuals and what is the most effective level of tailoring to use.

6.2.3 Taking forward the guidance on risk communication, usability and user testing and auditing the impact of the guidance

As well as completing the additional research set out above, it will also be important to audit the impact of the work of the Group and the guidance that has been produced to ensure that the expected improvements to PILs have actually occurred. The Group recommended that the following specific measures should be considered:

- to provide opportunities for the pharmaceutical industry to learn about the new initiatives described in this report and provide advice on their implementation. This process has already been started by the MHRA and the seminar to launch the Group's report will continue this process;

- to consult patient organisations in early 2006 to solicit views on current PILs for products for the conditions they cover and their adequacy to meet the needs of patients. Once feedback has been received, a meeting of patient representatives will be convened to discuss the findings, progress made and any further steps that should be taken to promote high quality PILs. As the improvements will take time to filter through, it is envisaged that this consultation process will need to be repeated in future years;

- in addition, the user test reports that have been submitted with applications to the MHRA will be audited to identify any common themes and difficulties where additional guidance or modification of existing guidance could be required;

- the MHRA will also collect and publish statistics and information on complaints about PILs received from the public. A facility for feedback on the quality of individual PILs will be included on the relevant section of the MHRA website.

All guidance documents will be kept under review and will be formally reviewed one year after implementation. Changes will be considered in the light of experience and, if appropriate, the Working Group and the CSM will be asked to advise on any proposed changes.

As part of a wider initiative on transparency, copies of currently approved PILs will be provided on the MHRA website as part of the assessment report. Initially this will cover all new medicines but it will also be extended to existing medicines over a period of time. The MHRA website will then become an additional source of the current PIL.

6.2.4 Publicity about the availability of PILs

Many people are unaware of the leaflet, or how to get one if it is not provided with their medicine, and do not appreciate its usefulness as a source of information about the medicine. The PIL can also be a helpful support to communication between patients and their healthcare providers. To coincide with the outcome of their work on a strategy to improve the quality of PILs, the Working Group advised that a publicity campaign should be devised by the Agency to alert patients and the public to the PIL and how it can be used to support the safe use of medicines.

The campaign should inform patients that they should receive a PIL with their medicine and provide advice on how to request one or access the information if a PIL has not been provided. The MHRA should also work with other stakeholders on how to alert groups with special needs, such as hospital patients and those receiving multiple medications repackaged together in dispensing packs without PILs, on how they can access information about the individual medicines they are receiving.

Secondly, the campaign should help patients to understand how they can use the PIL to obtain information about the safe use of their medicine(s) and where to go for further advice. This would tie in with the supplementary leaflet developed as part of the risk communication work in section 4.5.5. The publicity campaign may also be used to highlight the availability of alternative sources of information that may better meet their needs, as described in the information keys at Annex 6.

The campaign should target patients by a range of routes, including material for key websites such as the MHRA's, NHS Direct Online and Ask About Medicines Week and also leaflets and posters made available through pharmacies and doctors' surgeries. The MHRA will take forward these proposals as part of its public involvement strategy.

RECOMMENDATIONS

The impact of changes in the quality of PILs as a result of this report should be monitored with the aim of continual improvement, and the supporting guidelines periodically reviewed in the light of experience.

Further research should be undertaken on how to provide information in PILs that meets patients' needs in today's environment. In particular, this should explore improved communication of risks and benefits, and how information can promote safe and effective use of medicines by people with diverse needs.

Options should be explored for improved access to PILs, including availability at or before the prescription or purchase of a medicine, and in other situations where a PIL is not currently available.

Steps should be taken to promote wide public awareness of PILs and their availability in alternative formats. These should include publicity about the Group's leaflet on the risks and benefits of medicines.

GLOSSARY OF ACRONYMS

ADR   Adverse drug reaction

CSM   Committee on Safety of Medicines

DfES   Department for Education and Skills

DH   Department of Health

EU   European Union

MA   Marketing authorisation

MHRA   Medicines and Healthcare products Regulatory Agency

NAO   National Audit Office

NNH   Number needed to harm

NNT   Number needed to treat

OTC   Over the counter

PIL   Patient information leaflet

SPC   Summary of product characteristics

ANNEXES

1 List of members of the CSM Working Group on Patient Information and register of members interests

2 Terms of reference of the CSM Working Group on Patient Information

3 Response of the CSM Working Group on Patient Information to MHRA consultation on new legislation: MLX 309

4 Patient organisations consulted by the Working Group

5 Guidance on the user testing of patient information leaflets

6 Can you read the leaflet? A guideline on the usability of the patient information leaflet for medicinal products for human use

7 Report of a focus group discussion of the Seroxat patient information leaflet

8 Glossary of medical terms in lay language

9 Report of pilot testing of a leaflet on the risks and benefits of medicines

10 Guidance on communication of risk in patient information leaflets

ANNEX 1
LIST OF MEMBERS OF THE COMMITTEE ON SAFETY OF MEDICINES WORKING GROUP ON PATIENT INFORMATION

Ms Melinda Letts OBE – Chair
Immediate past Chair, Long-term Medical Conditions Alliance

Ms Helen Barnett BPharm MSc LicAc MBAcC
CSM Lay Representative

Dr Keith Beard BSc MB ChB FRCP (E) FRCP (G) FFPM
Consultant Physician, Medicine for the Elderly, Victoria Infirmary, Glasgow

Professor Dianne Berry D Phil C Psychol ACSS
Pro-Vice Chancellor Research & Professor of Psychology, Reading University

Professor Alison Blenkinsopp BPharm PhD MRPharmS (until January 2005)
Director of Education & Research & Regional Pharmaceutical Advisor, Department of Medicines Management, Keele University

Dr Katherine Darton BA BSc PhD LGSM
Mind

Mrs Helen Darracott LLB BPharm MRPharmS
Director of Legal & Regulatory Affairs, Proprietary Association of Great Britain

Mr David Dickinson MA FRSA
Principal Consultant, Consumation

Ms Jackie Glatter
Senior Public Affairs Consultant, Consumers' Association

Dr Nicola Gray PhD MRPharmS
Lecturer in Pharmacy Practice, The Pharmacy School, University of Nottingham

Ms Wendy Harris MRPharmS
Senior Pharmacist, National Patient Safety Agency

Professor Jennifer Hunt Hon D.Sci, M. Phil BA (Hons) RGN FRCN
Research Consultant

Dr Rosemary Leonard MA MB, BChir MRCGP DRCOG MBE
Principal in General Practice, London

Mr Dinesh Mehta BPharm MSc FRPharmS
Executive Editor of the British National Formulary

Ms Kristin McCarthy BA MA (Medical Law & Ethics)
Director, Developing Patient Partnerships

Ms Eileen Neilson BSc MSc
Head of Policy Development, Royal Pharmaceutical Society of Great Britain

Professor Theo Raynor BPharm (Hons) PhD MRPharmS
Head, Pharmacy Practice and Medicines Management, Leeds University

Carolyn, Lady Roberts RGN RHV MSc
Trustee, The Ethox Foundation – Oxford Centre for Ethics and Communication in Healthcare Practice

Ms Joanne Shaw
Director, Medicines Partnership

Dr Patricia Wilkie PhD
CSM Lay Representative

Mr Paul Woods BPharm MRPharmS
Pharmacist, Association of the British Pharmaceutical Industry

MEMBERS OF THE CSM WORKING GROUP ON PATIENT INFORMATION HAVE DECLARED CURRENT PERSONAL AND NON PERSONAL INTERESTS AS FOLLOWS:

MEMBER	PERSONAL INTERESTS		NON PERSONAL INTERESTS		
	NAME OF COMPANY	NATURE OF INTEREST	NAME OF COMPANY	NATURE OF INTEREST	WHETHER CURRENT
Ms Melinda Letts (CHAIR)	ABPI	Short Consultancy re Ask About Medicines Week Health & Medicines Information Guide and Directory (Fees Paid)	ABPI	) Part-Funders of Ask	Yes
			Roche	) About Medicines Week	Yes
	European Medicines Group	Chairing a Meeting about Patient Information & advising on a report about the same February 2005 (Fee Paid)	MSD	)	Yes
			Lilly	)	Yes
	Wave Healthcare Communications	Preparation of Brief for Speakers at a Series of GP meetings about Patients' Demands on GPs, October 2004 (Fee Paid)			
Ms Helen Barnett	None		None		
Dr Keith Beard	None		Aventis	Single, non-personal lecture fee in 2003.	No
			Novartis Consumer Health SA	Travel expenses to attend one meeting of an expert working group in 2000.	No
Professor Dianne Berry	None		None		

MEMBER	PERSONAL INTERESTS		NON PERSONAL INTERESTS		
	NAME OF COMPANY	NATURE OF INTEREST	NAME OF COMPANY	NATURE OF INTEREST	WHETHER CURRENT
Professor Alison Blenkinsopp	Astra Zeneca	Fees (Specific)	Pfizer	Commissioned Research	Yes
	Boehringer Ingelheim	" (Specific)	Lundbeck	"	Yes
	Alpharma	"			
	Novartis Consumer Health				
	Boots Healthcare Int				
	Galdema	" (Specific)			
	Galpharm	" (Specific)			
	J & J MSD	" (Specific)			
	GSK	" (Specific)			
Dr Katherine Darton	None		None		
Mrs Helen Darracott	PAGB	Salary	None		
Mr David Dickinson	Astra Zeneca	Shareholder/fees Consultancy	MSD	) Supporters of Ask	No
		Project- New Leaflet for Inhaler Treatment	Eli Lilly	) About Medicines Week	
			Novartis	) 2004 while I was	
	GSK	Fee Paid Work	Pfizer	) Chairman	
	Alcon Laboratories	"	Roche	"	
	Bristol Myers Squibb	"	Organon	"	
	Gilead	"	ABPI	"	
	Merck Sharp & Dohme	"			
	Novartis	"			
	Roche	"			

MEMBER	PERSONAL INTERESTS		NON PERSONAL INTERESTS		
	NAME OF COMPANY	NATURE OF INTEREST	NAME OF COMPANY	NATURE OF INTEREST	WHETHER CURRENT
Ms Jackie Glatter	None		None		
Dr Nicola Gray	None		None		
Ms Wendy Harris	None		None		
Professor Jennifer Hunt	None		None		
Dr Rosemary Leonard	Lilly	Fees / Publicity work	None		
	GSK	Fees / Publicity work			
	Crookes Healthcare	Fees / Advertorials			
Ms Nicky Lilliott	ABPI	Salary	None		
	GSK	Shareholder			
Ms Kristin McCarthy	None		None		
Mr Dinesh Mehta	None		None		
Ms Eileen Neilson	None		None		

| MEMBER | PERSONAL INTERESTS | | NON PERSONAL INTERESTS | | |
	NAME OF COMPANY	NATURE OF INTEREST	NAME OF COMPANY	NATURE OF INTEREST	WHETHER CURRENT
Professor Theo Raynor	Association of Self Medication Industry (Australia)	Travel & Subsistence Expenses for Lecturing	Drug Information Association (US)	Research Grant	No
	European Medicines Group	Travel & Subsistence for EMG Meeting	Faraday Packaging Partnership	Consultancy	No
	PAGB	Travel & Subsistence for Lecturing			
	Medicines Information Project	Fees & Expenses for Consultancy			
	Luto Research Ltd. (user testing service on PILs for pharmaceutical companies)	Executive Chairman & shareholder			
	Clients: ALK- Abello AstraZeneca Baxter Galpharm Rosemont Winthrop				

MEMBER	PERSONAL INTERESTS		NON PERSONAL INTERESTS		
	NAME OF COMPANY	NATURE OF INTEREST	NAME OF COMPANY	NATURE OF INTEREST	WHETHER CURRENT
Ms Carolyn Roberts	None		None		
Ms Joanne Shaw	None		MSD	)	Yes
			Pfizer	)	No
			Lilly	) Sponsorship/Ask About	No
			Organon	) Medicines Week	No
			Roche	)	No
			Novartis	)	No
			GSK	Honorarium	Yes
			Janssen Cilag	Honorarium	No
			Pfizer	Educational Grant	Yes
			Roche	Honorarium	Yes
Dr Patricia Wilkie	None		None		
Mr Paul Woods	Astra Zeneca	Employee Salary, Expenses, Shareholder	None		

Members of the Working Group are required to comply with the Code of Practice for members of the Medicines Commission and Section 4 committees and sub-committees on declaration of interests.

ANNEX 2
TERMS OF REFERENCE OF THE COMMITTEE ON SAFETY OF MEDICINES WORKING GROUP ON PATIENT INFORMATION

REMIT

- **To advise on a strategy to improve the quality of information provided with medicines within the regulatory environment in order to meet patient needs.**

- **To propose criteria against which the quality of patient information can be assessed to assure the safe and appropriate use of the medicine and the process by which these will be monitored.**

- **To advise on key cases which could impact significantly on public health and which will set standards for other products.**

In particular the Group will undertake the following:

Improvement of quality

1   To consider and identify the optimal model for providing balanced information on medicines to patients within the current and future regulatory environment.

- To advise on the optimal use of user testing of patient information leaflets; to propose measures for assessment and data analysis; and to propose actions for improvement.

- To consider and identify options for improving the clarity of communication of risk of reactions, their frequency and severity as set out in patient information leaflets.

2   To propose options on increasing patient involvement in the design and content of the information in patient leaflets to provide improved education and safety.

3   To advise on issues relating to accessibility of authorised patient information to promote safe use of medicines, taking into account:

- people with special needs, minority groups and others for whom access to information is difficult; and

- the need for patients to have access to the current version of the PIL.

4   To identify other information sources and how best to use these to supplement the statutory information in meeting patients' needs and liaise and co-operate with other relevant CSM Working Groups.

5   To advise on a common strategy which will inform the UK position within Europe on patient information whether national, mutual recognition or centralised.

Case work

6   To advise the Licensing Authority on an ad hoc basis, on the quality of information provided in the patient information leaflet, where the provision of safety information for specific medicines is important for public health.

and

7   To submit annually a report on progress in respect of the above terms of reference to the CSM.

ANNEX 3

RESPONSE OF THE COMMITTEE ON SAFETY OF MEDICINES WORKING GROUP ON PATIENT INFORMATION TO MHRA CONSULTATION ON NEW LEGISLATION: MLX 309

The Working Group on Patient Information was set up to advise on improving the quality of information provided with medicines in order to meet the needs of patients. Our membership includes lay, professional and industry representatives with an interest in patient information. Details of our membership and terms of reference are provided at Annex 1 and Annex 2.

Our response to consultation MLX 309 relates to item II of the proposals on the obligation on marketing authorisation holders to ensure that patient information leaflets reflect the results of consultation with target patient groups and the changes to Articles 59(3) and 61(1) of Directive 2001/83/EC as amended.

Legislative changes

The Group has taken a close interest in the opportunities being presented by the changes to European legislation on the patient information leaflet (PIL). We have discussed in detail how the proposed changes to Article 59(3) can be implemented to provide the maximum benefit to patients. The associated change in the order of information in Article 61(3) will also help make it easier to locate the items of information on the leaflet that most concern patients. We consider that these key legislative changes can be used to drive significant improvements in the quality of PILs and their ability to meet the needs of patients.

We have heard from the MHRA Secretariat that, although the current European Readability Guideline includes recommendations on user testing, the results of user testing to support the information in the PIL have not been submitted with UK national applications for marketing authorisations.

User testing

The user test in its most common form seeks to identify the key items of information that a patient would be likely to need to find in the PIL to ensure safe use of the product and then tests whether users are able to find and interpret this information. We have drawn on the expertise of members of the Group to develop detailed guidance on user testing of PILs. This covers not only methods for how the user test should be carried out but also recommendations for when a user test will be required. However, we are very conscious that this is a developing field in the UK and our guidance clearly states that the precise details of the method are not prescriptive. We are keen to support innovation where this serves to improve quality.

In our view, the requirement to user test patient information leaflets will lead to significant improvements in these documents because companies will have to test whether the information is accessible and understandable to patients.

Conclusion

We welcome the proposal to implement these legislative changes at an early date. We are clear that the changes provide a significant benefit because they will improve the information provided to patients with their medicines. This in turn will protect public health and enhance patient safety. The earlier this is implemented the earlier these benefits will be seen by patients.

Early implementation will also set clear standards for how this requirement can be met but it was recognised that the possibility of subsequent further changes to meet European requirements might present problems for companies. While the Group did not wish companies to face unreasonable difficulties, the interests of patients were agreed to be paramount.

CSM Working Group on Patient Information
October 2004

ANNEX 4

PATIENT ORGANISATIONS CONSULTED BY THE WORKING GROUP

The Committee on Safety of Medicines Working Group on Patient Information and the MHRA held a meeting with patient, carer and voluntary organisations on 5 July 2004 as a first step to initiate patient involvement in their work. Notices of the meeting were disseminated through the Long-term Medical Conditions Alliance and through the Association of Chief Executives of Voluntary Organisations, and made available on the MHRA website.

Organisations and individuals who had had previous contact with the Agency through the Working Group were also invited personally.

The following groups were represented at the meeting or provided written comments on the materials:

Alzheimer's Society
APRIL, Adverse Psychiatric Reaction Information Link
Association of Prostate Patients in London and Essex
Asthma UK
DANDA, Developmental Adult Neuro-Diversity Association
DIPEx
Epilepsy Action
Fellowship of Depressives Anonymous
HEART UK
LMCA, Long-term Medical Conditions Alliance
Medicines Partnership
Mind
National Association for Premenstrual Syndrome
National Osteoporosis Society
NRAS, National Rheumatoid Arthritis Society
National Society for Epilepsy
Pemphigus Vulgaris Network
Rethink
Seroxat Users' Group
Social Audit
Terrence Higgins Trust

ANNEX 5
GUIDANCE ON THE USER TESTING OF PATIENT INFORMATION LEAFLETS

1   **Introduction**

From 1 July 2005 new legal provisions exist in the UK for patient information particularly in relation to involving patients in ensuring that the information provided is legible, clear and easy to use[1]. This guidance expands upon earlier guidance from the European Commission on user testing of patient information leaflets which has been in use since 1999[2] and in turn adapted aspects of the work by the Communication Research Institute of Australia[3] in this area. It is addressed to marketing authorisation holders and aims to:

- help you decide how and when to apply a user test to PILs which accompany medicines for which you are responsible

- provide information about one way of undertaking a user test

- offer advice on who should be involved in the test process.

2   **Legal Basis**

All medicines are required by European and UK law to be accompanied by a Patient Information Leaflet (PIL) setting out comprehensive information which is accessible to and understandable by those who receive it, so that they can use their medicine safely and appropriately[1].

European Law now states:

The package leaflet shall reflect the results of consultations with target patient groups to ensure that it is legible clear and easy to use[4]...The results of assessments carried out in cooperation with target patient groups shall also be provided to the competent authority[5].

3   **What User Testing Is**

Before undertaking a formal user test, you should ensure that at all stages of the development of the PIL the views of patients are considered.

The reason for user testing is to help produce a leaflet that most medicine users can use to take safe and accurate decisions about their medicines.

Diagnostic user testing of patient information leaflets was pioneered in Australia in the early 1990s[3], and was recommended in guidelines on Readability in Europe by the European Commission in 1999[2]. It is a performance based, flexible development tool which identifies barriers to people's ability to understand and use the information presented, and indicates problem areas which should be rectified. It is particularly useful as part of a leaflet development process. If testing reveals barriers to understanding, carefully considered changes to the leaflet will be needed to improve it.

4   MHRA's Criteria for Assessing PILs Which Have Been Subject to Consultation with Target Patient Groups

This guidance includes an appendix describing one method of diagnostic testing of PILs. This is included for illustrative purposes only, and other performance-based methods are equally valid.   In approving PILs, MHRA will not require any particular method of testing to have been used, but will look for evidence that people who are likely to rely on the leaflet can find and appropriately use the information.

As the MA holder, you are advised to ensure that you have:

- Clearly defined before the test what the **most important information** is – for example, what the medicine is for, the dosage and any significant side effects and warnings

- Reflected in the test sample **populations who are particularly likely to rely on the leaflet** for the medicine in question (these may include carers)

- Provided **credible evidence**, for example data gathered from test participants to a clear protocol

- Provided evidence that test participants can **find and appropriately use the information**.

Where it is intended to market a medicine in the UK, any user testing undertaken should be on the English language version of the patient information leaflet.

5   **When to Undertake a User Test**

- While user testing of PILs is in its infancy, MHRA expects all PILs submitted for approval to have been user tested unless the MA holder can provide a full justification for exemption.

- Exemption will depend on the submission of appropriate justification, which:

  - might include standard formats and company standard operating procedures (SOP) for writing and testing PILs (including those of commercial sub-contractors); and

  - must demonstrate that PILs prepared according to that company's SOP and in a proven leaflet format have performed satisfactorily in a valid user test as described above.

In the event of revision of a company's SOP, future applications may not be able to rely on tests for a similar PIL tested according to the old SOP.

Over time, as knowledge and experience grow, it is likely that not all PILs will need to be user tested. Rather, some PILs may be able to rely on testing applied to PILs for similar products. Examples of when this might be considered acceptable include:

- Line extensions for the same route of administration

- The same safety issues identified

- The same drug class

- The same pharmaceutical form

- The same patient population

- The same format of PIL.

Each case will be judged on its merits and more than one of the criteria above may apply.

- There will still be circumstances where a user test is always required. These are likely to include but will not be restricted to:

  - New chemical entities

  - Medicines which have undergone a change in legal status

  - Medicines with a novel presentation

  - Medicines with particularly critical safety issues.

MHRA reserves the right to request a user test where there is any doubt regarding the usability of the information presented with an application.

6   Implementation

■ All applications which include a PIL and are submitted for assessment to the MHRA will be considered against the criteria in section 4 of this document.

■ The guidance affects all new applications for marketing authorisations submitted on or after **1 July 2005** which are affected by The Medicines (Marketing Authorisations and Miscellaneous Amendments) Regulations [SI 2004/3224.] This will apply in all areas of MHRA work (new MAs, PLPIs and herbals).

■ There will be a transitional period for existing marketing authorisation holders to comply with the new requirements. Applications in these circumstances will be submitted directly to the Product Information Unit.

■ There will be a final date for all leaflets to comply with requirements to reflect user testing and the changes in the order of the information presented, by **1 July 2008**.

■ Assessment policy will be to expect user testing to have been undertaken and the data to be submitted as part of the application or for a full justification for the absence of the test to be provided by the applicant.

Medicines and Healthcare products Regulatory Agency
June 2005

References

1. The Medicines (Marketing Authorisations and Miscellaneous Amendments) Regulations 2004 number 3224 [SI 2004/3224]

2. European Commission. Guideline on the Readability of the Label and Package Leaflet of Medicinal Products for Human Use. September 1998.

3. Sless D. & Wiseman R. *Writing about medicines for people: Usability Guidelines for Consumer Medicine Information* (2nd edition). Australian Government Publishing Service, Canberra. 1997

4. Title V of Council Directive 2001/83/EC (as amended), Article 59(3)

5. Title V of Council Directive 2001/83/EC (as amended), Article 61(1)

6. This guidance builds on experience gained with the European Guideline on the Readability of the Label and Package Leaflet of Medicinal Products for Human Use which adapted some aspects of the work by the Communication Research Institute of Australia.

APPENDIX
ILLUSTRATION – ONE WAY OF UNDERTAKING A TEST OF A PIL

The method described covers one-to-one, face-to-face, structured sets of interviews, involving at least 20 participants reflecting the population for whom the medicine is intended[6]. As indicated above, other performance-based methods are equally valid, and MHRA will judge applications on a case by case basis.

1 **Performing the test**

■ Testing of PILs may be done by the MA holder or a suitably qualified agency on its behalf.

■ It should be carried out by an experienced interviewer with good interview, observational and listening skills.

■ Ideally the writer of the PIL will carry out the interviews, or occasionally accompany the interviewer during testing, to enable direct transfer of learning.

2 **Recruiting Participants**

■ Ensure a range of different types of people who are able to imagine needing to use the medicine.

■ If the medicine is intended for a rare illness, then where possible test the leaflet among people who actually have the illness. You may need to exclude people who have previously taken or are currently taking the medicine.

■ Remember that information which can be used by the least able will be beneficial for all users. Try and include:

– particular age groups such as young people and older people – especially if the medicine is particularly relevant to their age group

– new users or people who do not normally use medicines, particularly for information provided with new medicines likely to be used by a wide range of people (e.g. analgesics or antihistamines)

– people who do not use written documents in their working life

– people who find written information difficult.

■ Recruit participants from wherever is most relevant and practical. For example you could use:

- older people's lunch clubs

- self-help groups

- patient support groups

- community centres

- parent and toddler groups.

■ If you use the NHS to identify subjects or provide premises, you will have to get ethical approval.

3   Sample Size and Use

■ Only small numbers of participants are needed. The aim is to meet the success criteria in a total of 20 participants. The important thing is not to re-test participants whom you have already tested. You can achieve this by undertaking:

- A pilot of around 3-6 participants to test that the questions will work in practice. As you gain experience, you may be able to use just two or three participants in the pilot test

- Next, at least two rounds of 10 people each, reviewing the results after the first round and making any necessary amendments to the PIL

- Repeat tests until you have satisfactory data from a group of 10 participants

- A final test of a further 10 to see if the success criteria are also met in this further 10 (i.e. in 20 participants in total).

4   Success Criteria

A satisfactory test outcome for the method outlined above is when 90% of literate adults are able to find the information requested within the PIL, of whom 90% can show that they understand it.

If you use a different method of testing, different success criteria may be appropriate. MHRA will consider these on a case-by-case basis.

5   Test Protocol

- ■ You are advised to:

  - – Draw up a new protocol for each product

  - – Include questions that address all the important and difficult issues, and use rigorous assessment criteria

  - – Include a set of expected correct answers

  - – Design the test to last no more than 45 minutes, to avoid tiring participants

  - – Ensure that the questions reflect any specific safety and compliance issues related to the medicine being tested. Testing is most beneficial when the questions relate to areas where patients' fears are greatest, such as side effects. Avoiding serious safety issues with a medicine during user testing of the PIL would invalidate the test.

- ■ The interviewer should:

  - – Use a written set of questions for reference

  - – Ask the questions orally

  - – Adopt a conversational manner, allowing ample opportunity for interaction with the participant

  - – Ask participants, once they have located the required information, not to repeat it parrot-fashion but to put it into their own words where appropriate

  - – As well as recording the answers to the questions, observe how each participant handles the leaflet and searches for information, noting, for example, whether people become lost or confused. This will yield valuable information about how to improve the structure of the PIL.

- ■ The questions should:

  - – Adequately cover any critical safety issues with the medicine.

  - – Be kept to a minimum; usually 12 -15 will be enough, though more may be required in special cases, e.g. if there are significant safety issues to be investigated

  - – Cover a balance of general and specific issues. A general issue might be what to do if a dose is missed, while a specific issue might relate to a side effect that occurs particularly with that medicine.

– Be phrased differently from the text of the leaflet to avoid "copy-cat" answers, based merely on identifying groups of words

– Appear in a random order (i.e. not in the order the information appears in the leaflet).

Copies of the protocol(s) including the questions asked, the responses offered, the interviewer's written observations and the different versions of the PIL tested must be submitted to the MHRA for review.

ANNEX 6

CAN YOU READ THE LEAFLET?
A GUIDELINE ON THE USABILITY OF THE PATIENT
INFORMATION LEAFLET FOR MEDICINAL
PRODUCTS FOR HUMAN USE

1   PURPOSE OF THIS GUIDELINE

This guideline is written to assist Marketing Authorisation (MA) holders when drawing up the PIL which accompanies the medicines for which they are responsible.   It sets out what you are expected to do to ensure the readability of the text for all patients from **1 July 2005** (see section 8 below). In addition to discussing the factors which influence readability of written documents generally, the guidance goes on to look at ways in which MA holders can make the statutory information available in formats suitable for particular patient populations who may be unable to access the information routinely provided, and gives suggestions for how best to meet their needs.

2   LEGAL BASIS

All medicines are required by European and UK law to be accompanied by a Patient Information Leaflet (PIL) setting out comprehensive information which is accessible to and understandable by those who receive it, so that they can use their medicine safely and appropriately.[1]

European law now states as follows:

"The package leaflet must be written and designed to be clear and understandable, enabling users to act appropriately, when necessary with the help of health professionals. The package leaflet must be clearly legible in the official language or languages of the member state in which the medicinal product is placed on the market." [2]

Following recent changes in the European law on medicines information, PILs in the UK must, from July 2005, be user-tested and the result of such user testing must be submitted to the MHRA. This is the subject of separate guidance.[3]

The review of medicines legislation also includes the following new provision:

"The MAH shall ensure that the package information leaflet is made available on request from patients' organisations in formats appropriate for the blind and partially sighted."[4]

Guidance on this issue has been developed at a European level and published in the Commission's *Guidance concerning the Braille requirements for labelling and the package leaflet.*[5]

3   BACKGROUND

For the majority of medicine users, a well written, clearly designed PIL can be an important source of information about their medicines. Earlier guidance from Europe[6] made reference to the factors which influence the clarity and accessibility of the information presented. In developing this guidance document these factors have been elaborated upon and expanded to give more detailed advice on how best to produce clear and well designed leaflets. Guidance is also provided on how to ensure that blind and partially sighted medicine users are provided with the statutory information in a format suited to their needs and preferences.

Additionally the new legal obligations in relation to blind and partially sighted medicine users provide an opportunity for considering other patient and carer populations who may benefit from being able to access the statutory information in an alternative format. This will ensure that as many people as possible are able to access the information and use their medicines safely and effectively. To this end, a set of information keys has been developed to help MA holders review their products and determine which particular formats or ways of delivering the information would be of assistance to people with specific needs among their target user populations.

There are some medicine users who do not find it easy to read and interpret information, including some people for whom English is a second language and people with poor basic skills in reading, numeracy and language use. Children who take medicines and their parents, and carers who help others to take medicines, may also have information needs for which the standard PIL does not cater. The information keys are designed to ensure that these and other people with particular needs can make full use of the information provided. It is important to bear in mind that these are not discrete groupings within the population and individuals may have multiple needs.

4 TEMPLATES

Templates will help to ensure that the statutory information appears as intended by the Directive. The use of templates could also ensure consistency in the information provided across a number of different medicines. Using a template structure will provide a harmonised means of presenting the information in the correct order. It should not be used as an argument for not undertaking a user test or other form of user consultation.

5 PRODUCING CLEAR LEAFLETS – FACTORS TO CONSIDER

If PILs are well designed and clearly worded, this maximises the number of people who can use the information, including older children and adolescents, those with limited English or poor literacy skills and those with some degree of sight loss. Companies are encouraged to seek advice from specialists in information design when devising their house style for PILs to ensure that the design aids navigation and access to information.

5.1 Choosing a writing style

- Bear in mind many people trying to read the leaflet may have poor reading skills. More are likely to have poor health literacy. Aim to use simple words of few syllables. Avoid Latinate words, eg use 'understand' rather than 'comprehend'.

- Punctuation should be simple. Sentences should be no more than about 20 words. It is better to use a couple of sentences rather than one longer sentence, especially for new information.

- Long paragraphs can confuse readers, particularly where lists of side effects are included. The use of bullet points for such lists gives a more open approach. Five or six bullet points in a list should be the maximum.

5.2 Choosing a Typeface

- **Choose a font which is easy to read.** For large quantities of text such as that found in PILs, a serif typeface is preferred since the shape of the characters is easier to read. Most books are set in semi-bold serif typefaces whereas bold sans serif fonts are more often used for signs. Stylised fonts such Johannes or Flamenco are difficult to read and should not be used. It is important to choose a typeface in which similar letters, such as "i" and "l", can be easily distinguished from each other.

■ **Make your font size generally 14 point for headings and 12 point for the main body of the text.** Consideration should be given to using larger fonts where it is known that patients with visual impairment are likely to be using the PIL, for example PILs supplied with eye drops. For visually impaired patients the preferred font size should be between 16 and 20.

■ **The widespread use of capitals should be avoided.** The human eye recognises words in written documents by the word shape, so choose lower case text for large blocks of text.

■ **Do not use italic fonts and underlining** as they make it harder for the reader to recognise the word shape.

5.3 Design and Layout of the Information

■ **Set all text horizontally.**

■ **Keep line spaces clear.** The space between lines is an important factor influencing the clarity of the text. As a general rule the space between one line and the next should be at least 1.5 times the space between words on a line.

■ **Pay attention to spacing.**

Keep line length to between 60-70 characters per line unless using columns. Leave spaces between paragraphs to rest the eye (white space within the document is also important as a reading aid). Keep the word spacing consistent throughout the document. Align the text to the left margin to aid location of the start of each line of text. Do not use "justified" or "centred" text as they are not easy to read since word spacing varies.

■ **Contrast between the text and the background is important.** Factors to bear in mind include paper weight, size and weight of the type, colour of the type and colour of the paper itself. Too little contrast between the text and the background adversely affects the accessibility of the information. So avoid background images behind the text which will interfere with the clarity of the information and make it harder to read. Glossy paper reflects light, making the information difficult to read, so choose uncoated paper. The paper weight is important because show-through of text impairs legibility.

■ **A column format for the text can help the reader navigate the information.** Remember to make sure that the margin between the columns is large enough to adequately separate the text. If space is limited use a vertical line to separate the information. Keep important information together so the text flows easily from one column to the next.

5.4   Headings

- **Headings** are an important aspect of the written information and, if well used, can help patients navigate the text.

- Use **bold text** or different colours for headings, to help make them stand out.

- **Make sure headings are consistently placed** and use **consistent font** types and sizes.

- **Using lines** to separate the different sections within the text can also be helpful as a navigational tool.

5.5   Use of Colour

- **Colour can help** readers navigate the PIL.

- **Contrast is important,** and the relationship between the colours used is as important as the colours themselves.

- As a general rule **dark text** should be contrasted against a **light background.**

- There may be occasions when **reverse type** may be used to highlight particular warnings.   In such circumstances the quality of the print will need careful consideration and may require the use of a larger font or bold text. Reversed-out text is particularly difficult for older readers.

5.6   Use of Symbols and Pictograms

The legal provisions within article 62 of Council Directive 2001/83/EC (as amended) permit the use of images, pictograms and other graphics to aid comprehension of the information.

- Symbols and pictograms can be useful **provided the meaning of the symbol is clear** and the size of the graphic makes it easily legible.

- **User testing of all symbols will be important** to ensure the meaning is generally understood.

6 PROVIDING THE LEAFLET IN OTHER FORMATS

6.1 Different formats for blind and partially sighted people

Many people who cannot read the PIL could access the information if the PIL were provided in another format. The new legal provisions require MA holders to provide the statutory information in a format suitable for blind and partially sighted medicine users. This can be achieved in a number of ways and what is provided will depend on user preference. You should ensure that you are able to provide the statutory information in any format which may be requested on behalf of the user.

- **Large print versions** of the leaflet would help many people with sight loss. They may also be easier to read for some people with learning difficulties. Individuals have different preferences, so it is probably more useful to have the facility to print in a range of font sizes than to choose a single option. The usual range of font sizes is 16-24 using a clear font which is either roman, semibold or bold.

- **Audiotape or CD versions** of the leaflet can help people with sight loss, those with limited command of English who can understand the spoken word better than written text and people with reading or learning difficulties.

- **Braille versions** can be useful for the approximately 20,000 Braille readers in the UK. Separate guidance on the provision of leaflets in Braille is available from the European Commission, and the UK will develop its own supplementary guidance to help MA holders meet this obligation nationally.

- **Electronic versions** of the leaflet include email and Microsoft Word documents which can be sent on floppy disk, CD-ROM, attached to an email or downloaded from a website. These can be useful for blind or partially sighted people and others who use a computer with text-to-speech or screen magnification software, or other 'access technology' devices. Website standards are available to ensure that the format of the material is suitable for use with the access technologies referred to above.

Some leaflets are currently available from the Electronic Medicines Compendium (www.medicines.org.uk - restricted format in many cases) or from company websites.

Information on standards for the provision of information in each of these alternative formats is provided by:

(i) RNIB - Royal National Institute of the Blind   www.rnib.org.uk

The RNIB See It Right Pack provides advice on a wide range of alternative formats to make information accessible to those with sight loss.

6.2   Making alternative formats available

■   Signposting in the PIL

The most obvious way of making people aware of the availability of alternative formats of the leaflet is to include a clear statement in the PIL. Place this prominently in the leaflet in at least 14 point bold text.

Possible wordings include:

"Is this leaflet hard to see or read? Phone 0123 456789 for help"
"Reading or sight problems? Call 0123 456789 for help"
"For information in large print, tape, CD or Braille, phone 0123 456789"
"Call 0123 456789 for a leaflet in large print, tape, CD or Braille"
"Hard to read? Call 0123 456789 for help"

Make sure that the meaning is understood and that the positioning and design helps patients to find it. This can be achieved by user testing[3].

6.3   Fulfilling orders for alternative formats

The helpline number may be that of a company Medical Information Department or a third party contractor under a service agreement. Make sure that there is appropriate quality assurance checking so that the current PIL is provided.

The PIL supplied in alternative format must be identical to the currently approved PIL. To avoid confusion, companies may need to have in place measures to explain why there may appear to be differences if a PIL has recently been updated.

Medicine users' individual requirements and preferences differ, so you may find it easier to have the resources available to prepare PILs in alternative formats on demand rather than holding a store in several different formats which would become obsolete whenever any change is made to the PIL.

You must not use any information about consumers gained by this means for other purposes.

7. THE INFORMATION KEYS

Clear PILs will help many people to use their medicines safely and appropriately. These information keys are provided to help MA holders make information on the safe use of their medicines available in forms accessible to people who cannot use or get the best from the standard PIL.

You are encouraged to use this guidance to identify measures that will promote access to the information in the PIL for specific sectors of the population who are likely to use your medicines, and to have the facilities to make PIL information available in a number of formats to suit the needs of the particular user.

The keys can be used to identify tailored options for specific products where a significant proportion of users are likely to have difficulty in accessing the information in the PIL. In considering what would be the most helpful for a particular medicine you should consider:

■ Which disease(s) is the medicine used to treat?

Will a high proportion of users have difficulty in reading the PIL? An example would be a product for the treatment of glaucoma, for which a significant proportion of the patient population would be likely to be those with some degree of sight loss.

■ Who will use the medicine?

Are there particular groups with special needs who form a significant proportion of those using the product? Examples could include a product for a condition prevalent in elderly people from ethnic minorities who may have limited command of English, a product for dementia likely to be regularly administered by carers or a product indicated for use in older children.

This is not an exhaustive list and you are encouraged to think around the problem and consider other alternative and innovative solutions.

(i) **Patient organisations** are often very experienced in providing materials in alternative formats that can be readily accessed by people with special needs. You should consider consulting relevant patient groups on the most helpful options and how they could be presented, as well as working with patients to develop the PIL.

The table overleaf can be used to help identify which options may be most useful for the particular target populations identified. Remember that individuals may have multiple needs.

Some of these options have already been discussed at 6 above in relation to provision of information for blind and partially sighted people.

Table 1 – Toolkit of options to help specific groups

Note: Target groups may contain individuals in more than one category. For example, a carer may also have limited English.

Target group	Information key							
	Large print	Audiotape/CD	Braille	Electronic versions	Translated PILs	Infomediaries	Helplines	Additional materials
Sight loss	✓✓✓	✓✓✓	✓✓	✓✓	–	✓✓✓	✓✓✓	✓✓
Poor basic skills	✓	✓✓✓	–	✓	–	✓✓✓	✓✓✓	✓✓
Limited English	–	✓✓	–	✓	✓✓✓	✓✓✓	✓✓	✓
Children	–	✓	–	✓✓	–	✓✓	✓	✓✓✓
Carers	–	–	–	✓	–	✓✓	✓✓	✓✓✓

Key: ✓✓✓ highly recommended   ✓✓ recommended for certain groups/in some circumstances   ✓ may be useful   not specifically recommended for this group

7.1 Identifying people who need information in alternative formats

▪ Pharmacists and other health professionals

Pharmacists are in a good position to identify and guide people who need help with information, when they are collecting prescriptions (although prescriptions may be collected by a representative). Prescribers and nurse-led and other specialist support services may also be in a position to identify special needs for information.

As technology becomes more widely available in pharmacies, pharmacists may also be able to access services (eg web-based information) on behalf of the medicine user and help them access information in a format tailored to their needs.

- ▪ **Information leaflets and posters** in pharmacies and surgeries are another way of alerting people to the availability of PILs in different formats.

- ▪ **Signposting in the PIL** is described in Section 6.2

- ▪ **Patient organisations and NHS Direct** may also have a role in publicising the availability of information in alternative formats. You are also encouraged to consider other ways in which people can be made aware of what is available. For OTC products, details may be included in advertising.

7.2 Providing the PIL in other languages

The PIL must be written in the official language of the member state (for the UK this is English) although other languages may be used as well, provided that the same particulars appear in all languages used.

- ▪ **A leaflet in another language** may benefit people with limited command of English. This option is especially relevant where a disease is particularly prevalent in certain ethnic populations.

A faithful translation of the English version must be obtained. This need not be verbatim but must adequately convey the intended messages. When commissioning translations you should verify the quality standards of translation services.

7.3 'Infomediaries'

'Infomediaries' act as intermediates to facilitate the provision of information to people with special access needs. For example, an infomediary may read and explain the PIL to someone who cannot read the printed version.

- **Helplines**, which may take the form of recorded information or a live advice service, can help most people with special access needs. They are already widely used and supported. Where a helpline is publicised in a PIL, a copy of the script or the recorded information should be provided to the MHRA Product Information Unit in advance to ensure that the content complies with the legal requirements.

You can also alert patients to the availability of helplines through material provided to prescribers or other health professionals. This is less likely to reach patients as it relies on memory and availability at the time of consultation. For OTC products, details may also be included in advertising.

- **Translation services** can help people who cannot read English. A proposal for NHS Direct to develop this service is included in the Department of Health Information Strategy[7]. Some patient groups can help people who speak other languages. Where available, it may be helpful to highlight translation services in the PIL.

- **Navigators** to help people access information are also proposed in the Information Strategy[7]. They may have a role in interpreting the information in the PIL for people who need such help, and further information will be included in future editions of this guidance as this service is developed and piloted. NHS Direct may have a role here.

7.4 Accessing additional information

- **Pointers to information sources**

One PIL will not be sufficient to meet the information needs of all the diverse patients who receive a medicine. Further information about the medicine may be provided by a number of means and the PIL may serve as a pointer to sources of further information as well as to patient organisations and other sources of further support to patients and carers.

Suggested wordings could include "For further information, go to …" or "If you want to know/find out more, go to …". Depending on the product, this may then lead to a patient organisation, the Ask About Medicines portal and Health & Medicines Guide & Directory, company support service, NHS Direct online or the Consumer Health Information Centre.

- **Patient organisations** are a valuable source of further information about diseases and their management and treatment. They often run helplines and have a range of paper and website based information resources to support patients.

It is permissible to include details of a relevant patient organisation in the PIL.

■ **Additional leaflets** are not precluded by the legislation where these could be of benefit, such as a leaflet for carers or for children prescribed a medicine. These cannot be provided in the pack, but a reference to their availability could be placed in the PIL. Companies often also provide additional patient support materials to prescribers to pass on to their patients but this relies on memory and availability at the time of consultation. Such materials must always be non-promotional.

Before designing an additional leaflet, companies should identify whether the desired outcome can be achieved by simplifying the existing PIL without loss of information or by providing additional information in the PIL that would be of use to patients and carers.

■ **Simplified leaflets** may help people with literacy or learning difficulties or limited command of English. They may also help older children to understand how to use their medicine.

■ **Videos** are likely to be of most use in helping to explain complex instructions such as how to take an inhaled medicine or prepare a complex product.

■ **Booklets** can provide additional information, such as disease awareness material or information targeted at particular groups, but consideration should always be given to whether the information could be included in the PIL as that is more likely to reach the user.

■ **Magazines** can help to support people who use a medicine long-term. There must always be a clear procedure to unsubscribe for repeat materials.

■ **Websites** can provide a source of additional information and information in alternative forms. NHS Direct Online and linked sites are a particularly good resource. Currently European law prohibits the citing of website addresses in the PIL, for reasons including the need to ensure that material is consistent with the PIL.

ⓘ RNIB Web Access Centre provides useful advice on testing the accessibility of website information and links to other services. This is available from:

http://www.rnib.org/xpedio/groups/public/documents/publicwebsite/public_tools.hcsp

(i) Health on the Net (HON) Foundation (www.hon.ch)

This organisation provides advice and accreditation of website material under the HONCode.

As part of the Information Strategy[7], DH and NHS Direct are working on an information accreditation scheme which may be used for this type of material.

- **Digital TV** is being piloted by the Department of Health as a source of health information and it is likely that in the future this will be a source of additional information about medicines.

(i) Other sources of advice and support on writing health information

Plain English campaign (www.plainenglish.co.uk)
This group offers advice and guidelines and can apply their quality 'Crystal Mark'.

Communication Research Institute of Australia (www.communication.org.au)
A book, *Writing about medicines for people* by D Sless & R Wiseman, is available from this site. It draws on Australian experience of writing consumer medicines information. The website also lists other relevant Australian guidance.

Consumer Health Information Consortium (CHIC) (www.omni.ac.uk/CHIC/)
This is an autonomous UK organisation run by and for people interested in the provision of high quality health information to the public. The website includes a list of resources on producing information, accessibility and quality assessment.

Duman, M (2003) *Producing Patient Information.* London, Kings Fund. ISBN 1857174704. £20, available from the Kings Fund Online bookshop [available only in print].

8 **IMPLEMENTATION**

All applications submitted for assessment to the MHRA which include a PIL will be considered against the criteria in this document.   The guidance affects all new applications for marketing authorisations submitted on or after **1 July 2005** which are affected by The Medicines (Marketing Authorisations and Miscellaneous Amendments) Regulations 2004 [SI 2004/3224].   This will apply in all areas of MHRA work (new MAs, PLPIs and herbals). There will be a transitional period for existing marketing authorisation holders to take this guidance into account. When proposing changes to the order of the information and other significant changes to the leaflet, applications will need to be submitted directly to the Product Information Unit. There will be a final date for all leaflets to comply with requirements to reflect usability by **1 July 2008**. Assessment policy will be to expect all aspects of usability to have been considered by the applicant unless justified.

**Medicines and Healthcare products Regulatory Agency
June 2005**

References

1. Title V of Council Directive 2001/83/EC (as amended) covers the information to be included on the labelling and within the PIL of all medicines.   Article 59 sets out the information which must be contained within the PIL and the order in which this information must appear.

2. Title V of Council Directive 2001/83/EC (as amended) Article 63(2).

3. MHRA Guidance on the User Testing of Patient Information Leaflets.

4. Title V of Council Directive 2001/83/EC (as amended) Article 56.

5. European Commission. *Guidance concerning the Braille requirements for labelling and the package leaflet.* 2005.

6. This guidance builds on experience gained with the European Guideline on the Readability of the Label and Package Leaflet of Medicinal Products for Human Use.

7 Department of Health. *Better information, better choices, better health: Putting information at the centre of health.* London. December 2004.

ANNEX 7
REPORT OF THE FOCUS GROUP ON THE SEROXAT PIL

Medicines and Healthcare products Regulatory Agency

Safeguarding public health

Committee on Safety of Medicines
Working Group on Patient Information

Report on a focus group discussion of the Seroxat patient information leaflet
Wednesday 13 October 2004 at 14:30 at Market Towers

Facilitator:

Mary Chambers, Chief Nurse and Professor of Mental Health Nursing at South West London & St Georges' Mental Health NHS Trust and a member of the SSRI Working Group of the Committee on Safety of Medicines

Attendees:

Representatives from patient interest and user groups and MHRA Product Information Unit/Post Licensing Assessment Group.

Aim:

The aim of this focus group was to obtain the views of attendees on a revised patient information leaflet (PIL) for Seroxat (paroxetine) and whether this meets the needs of users for written information provided with the medicine.

Methodology:

All sections of the PIL were reviewed to identify any areas where the information needs to be clarified to ensure that the key messages are understood. Any omissions that need to be included in the PIL were flagged. Time did not permit consideration of the validity of the questions asked in the company-sponsored user test undertaken previously on the PIL.

THE SEROXAT PATIENT INFORMATION LEAFLET

Summary/Index "In this leaflet":

Proposed additions to the PIL:

■ The primary warnings to allow patients to make an informed choice in terms of the harm to benefit should be in larger print at the top of the PIL either in a "Warning" category or in a black box. This should concentrate on:

1. the dose-related adverse effects;

2. the withdrawal effects (understanding the withdrawal symptoms will help the patient cope better);

3. the risks during pregnancy (particularly hypoxic incidents during the third trimester);

4. the advice on what to do if "…you miss a dose" should be stronger and perhaps also appear in the black box area as a warning.

■ Clear and consistent labelling, whether called Seroxat or paroxetine throughout.

Discussion points:

■ Suicidal ideation and the risk of suicide or self-harm, regardless of cause, is more likely to occur in the 18-29 year age group. [Members of the group commented that suicidal ideation and akathisia can happen within a short time of initiating treatment, with a sudden change in the dose, or as a consequence of missing a dose or on drug withdrawal].

■ Is the balance right – would it be helpful to give element of the benefits as well as the risks?

■ Accessibility of the PIL to all patients. The doctor's consultation is not long enough and some patients will have difficulty reading and understanding the PIL.

■ Empower patients by giving them enough information up-front for them to make an informed choice (can they handle it?) but also that they can seek advice from their pharmacist if they are still unsure.

Section 1 "What Seroxat is and what it is used for":

Discussion points:

■ The accuracy of the information in this section was questioned. Does Seroxat selectively increase serotonin levels in the brain? Does Seroxat really alleviate depression or can it make it worse? How much of the effect is "placebo"?

■ Although patients are advised in the summary section that "If after a couple of weeks you don't start to feel better, go back to your doctor", often all the doctor will do is advise an increase in the dose. That a patient is feeling worse should not always be a reason to increase the dose but rather may be due to drug intolerance and that increasing the dose may not produce improvement.

Section 2 "Before you take Seroxat":

Proposed addition to the PIL:

■ Patients should be encouraged to also tell a relative or close friend that they are taking this medicine and even ask them to read the PIL (and any other information that has been provided).

Discussion point:

■ The prescriber needs to support the patient through all phases of treatment. This is particularly important when the patient first starts taking the medicine.

In the "Check with your doctor" section:

Proposed additions to the PIL:

■ "Are you taking other medicines?" [Link a cross-reference to the "other medicines and Seroxat" section].

■ "Are you pregnant or planning to become pregnant?"

■ "…or have you ever experienced a psychiatric adverse effect (mental illness) whilst taking any other medicine" to the statement "Do you suffer from episodes of mania (overactive behaviour or thoughts)?"

Discussion point:

■ If the patient is pregnant, they should be referred to a specialist in pre-natal depression. The group discussed whether women of child-bearing age should be precluded from taking Seroxat.

On the "Thoughts of harming yourself" section:

Discussion point:

■ A question was raised as to whether the statement "These may be increased when you first start taking antidepressants since these medicines take time to work" is valid since such thoughts may occur:

■ when your dose is changed;

■ when you stop taking this medicine or miss a dose (see Section 5, withdrawal effects).

In "Seroxat and alcohol":

Proposed addition to the PIL:

■ It would be helpful to state "You should not drink…" and explain reasons why ie:

■ the effect on liver enzymes (thus increasing or decreasing drug efficacy or the risk of drug toxicity or both);

■ enhancing the depressant effects of alcohol and

■ increasing the risk of experiencing adverse effects.

rather than the current bald "Do not drink alcohol while you are taking Seroxat" statement. Would a small amount of alcohol be acceptable? Giving the reasons allows for informed choice.

Section 3 "How to take your tablets":

Proposed additions to the PIL:

■ The "side effects" if a dose is missed, should be referred to as "withdrawal effects". It may be helpful to cross-refer to the section containing information on the withdrawal effects. The advice on what to do if "…you miss a dose" should be stronger and perhaps also appear in the black box area as a warning.

■ It was considered helpful to include "first aid" information for what to do if someone takes more than they should so that anyone can help. Not all hospitals are prepared for patients who have overdosed so perhaps to have this information available on the website.

Discussion points:

- The importance of the patient drinking water and keeping hydrated throughout the day would be useful additional information.

- The importance of dose-titration was raised especially as this can alleviate symptoms when initiating treatment. The minimal dose should always be considered to be the optimal dose. The emphasis is currently on the doctor increasing the dose rather than telling the patient that the dose could also be reduced and that they should speak to their doctor about it.

- The patient should also be prescribed the lowest strength pack rather than a higher strength and expected to halve tablets. [Problems with halving tablets].

- Although patients are advised in the summary section that "If after a couple of weeks you don't start to feel better, go back to your doctor", often all the doctor will do is advise an increase in the dose. That a patient is feeling worse should not always be a reason to increase the dose but rather may be due to drug intolerance and that increasing the dose may not produce improvement.

Section 4 "Possible side effects":

Proposed changes to the PIL:

- Change the headings from frequency to the actual adverse effects and have statistics under headings.

- The common side effects should be listed.

Discussion points:

- Most adverse drug reactions (ADRs) that occur are dose-related.

- A comment was made that the side effects should be called "adverse effects" but it was felt that "side effects" is the more generally recognised term.

- Concern was expressed that the product may be taken for its effects on erection and delayed ejaculation.

Section 5 "Stopping Seroxat":

Proposed changes to the PIL:

- Add "and the withdrawal effects" to the section title and replace "possible side effects" with "withdrawal effects" throughout this section and where it occurs elsewhere.

- As for section 4, describe the adverse effect first before indicating the frequency.

Discussion points:

- Many patients get withdrawal effects to a drug due to dependency, rather than from stopping the drug.

- To include information from (or at least encourage wider access and availability of) the "Protocol for the Withdrawal of SSRI Antidepressants" by Professor David Healy.

- The group supported the removal of information about placebo effects (included in a previous version of the PIL).

Section 6 "Children and adolescents under 18":

Proposed change to the PIL:

- Also that "(affecting less than 1 in 10)" should be highlighted in bold and underlined.

Discussion points:

- There was a question as to whether the statement "These studies also showed that the same symptoms...although these were seen less often" was appropriate, although the group was divided in opinion as to whether it should be removed.

- Listing the withdrawal effects separately from the adverse effects.

Section 7 "Looking after your tablets":

Discussion points:

- To emphasise (again) that the patient should keep the PIL to read again.

■ Regarding "…using half tablets…", there are problems with breaking the tablets and being able to store them appropriately that needs to be addressed.

■ Clarity and emphasis on the expiry date and where it appears.

Additional points raised:

■ A question of access to reports of suicidal ideation, suicide attempts and deaths recorded as being due to suicide.

■ There was a question regarding the packaging in terms of whether it should be child-resistant. Also the pack size of 30 tablets per prescription was considered too large. Individuals encouraged the use of some arrangements whereby pharmacists hold some medication back when filling a prescription so that the patient receives the prescription in instalments (as for an addiction).

■ A 7 tablet pack size was considered to be the most appropriate by some members of the group.

■ Warning to health professionals to monitor patients for worsening depression, regardless of the cause.

■ The provision of additional information:

■ The SPC should be provided to all prescribers,

■ General information pamphlet available to all patients about their illness,

■ More information to non-specialist prescribers e.g. GPs,

■ Guidance on dose adjustment, dependence and interactions for both patients and GPs.

■ In March 2004, the FDA issued Public Health Advisory ("Latest SSRI and similar antidepressants News Update") on cautions for use of antidepressants in adults and children. The FDA is asking manufacturers to change the labels of ten drugs to include stronger cautions of warnings about the need to monitor patients for the worsening of depression and the emergence of suicidal ideation, regardless of the cause of such worsening.

■ Is the MHRA considering taking similar action?

■ The risk of hypoxic incidents on induction of birth in the third trimester. The incidence and need for a warning was questioned.

Additional comments received in correspondence:

These comments are noted for the record but were not discussed specifically by the focus group other than as detailed above.

Section 2 "Before you take Seroxat":

- Responsibility of GPs to check what other medicines their patient is taking before prescribing Seroxat.

- A comment that Seroxat may cause anxiety and suicidal thoughts in all patients under and over 18, some of whom have never had these symptoms prior to being prescribed Seroxat/SSRIs. Why does the PIL say under 29 years old? Is there separate data for each age range and are the results available?

- There are existing reports that Seroxat/SSRIs cause harm to unborn babies and that babies suffer withdrawal from Seroxat/SSRIs at birth.

- Over the counter medicines such as decongestants also react badly with Seroxat. ECG readings can be affected by taking Seroxat.

- GPs need to be specifically aware of the effects of Seroxat combined with alcohol and warn patients appropriately when prescribing (not many do at the moment).

- GPs need to be specifically aware of the effects of Seroxat on driving and using machinery and warn patients appropriately when prescribing (not many do at the moment). The DoT and RAC have reported that the accident rate has increased because of people driving whilst taking SSRIs. If patients under 29 years old have to be closely monitored for suicidal tendencies during the first few weeks/months of treatment, then surely they should not be allowed to drive during this period.

Section 3 "How to take your tablets":

- Dose in depression: different opinions as to when the patient should start to feel a positive therapeutic effect and whether this is any better than placebo. It has been proven that suicidal tendency increases when the daily dose is more than 20 mg. Have the suicide rates for counties across England and also in prisons, in relation to antidepressants, been analysed. The suicide rate in prisons has risen over the last few years and for the elderly (in Herts) has risen dramatically in the last two years.

- Seroxat can cause OCD – a case is known where it occurred after a year of treatment and disappeared on stopping treatment.

- Many cases of panic attacks are experienced after taking Seroxat that had not occurred before.

- Seroxat can also cause liver problems and patients should be regularly monitored.

Section 4 "Possible side effects":

- Additional side effects in up to 1 in 10 people:

- Irregular heartbeat

- Excessive body heat

- Sensitivity to noise

- Gastrointestinal problems

- Bad memory

- Bad dreams

A comment that these effects can become worse on long-term treatment. These drugs were designed for short-term treatment of depression.

- Will patients read the entire list of side effects and manage to put themselves into a category. Why has the number of people experiencing side effects risen in the last 2 years? Until recently the PIL stated that only a few people would experience side effects. Some people may experience side effects for the duration of treatment.

Section 5 "Stopping Seroxat":

- The majority of GPs will wean patients off over 2 weeks, which is not long enough in most cases. GPs and hospital health professionals need to be better informed as to the withdrawal procedure. What guideline is currently issued to health professionals?

- "Withdrawal symptoms" should be named as such, not as "side effects when you are coming off…".

- "Less commonly" should be removed as the majority of people experience "electric shock sensations".

- Many people report arthritic problems on stopping Seroxat. GSK has acknowledged this but it still does not appear in the PIL.

■ Many patients have turned to groups such as the SeroxatUserGroup for advice on adverse and withdrawal effects because their GPs do not have the information or knowledge to advise patients. The symptoms experienced on withdrawal can mimic the original symptoms and GPs can misdiagnose and represcribe the drug by thinking the depression is returning.

■ Can patients be advised to ask their GP to fill out a yellow card on their behalf, if they experience adverse or withdrawal effects?

Section 6 "Children and adolescents under 18":

■ If the withdrawal effects have been found to be the same in 18-19 age group as adults then why are the suicidal tendencies/side effects/withdrawal symptoms not the same? What is the difference between a 29 year old, being at risk of suicidal thoughts/suicide, and a 32 or 40 year old, or any other age?

Conclusion:

MHRA thanked participants for their contribution to the discussion on the Seroxat PIL. The next step is for the CSM Expert Working Group on the Safety of SSRIs to review the key comments and concerns raised and to discuss what implications they have for the current draft of the Seroxat PIL. The Expert Working Group's recommendations will then be communicated to GSK as appropriate.

MHRA
November 2004

ANNEX 8
GLOSSARY OF MEDICAL TERMS IN LAY LANGUAGE

The CSM Working Group on Patient Information recognises that users may not be familiar with the terms used in patient information leaflets to describe unwanted effects of a medicine.

In order to promote consistency and to aid production of clear and understandable leaflets, the MHRA and the Working Group have developed the attached list of medical terms with suggested wording suitable for lay readers to describe possible adverse effects of a medicine. The list is not comprehensive and further terms will be added in the future.

Term	Proposed lay term
Agranulocytosis	Severe reduction in the number of white blood cells which makes infections more likely.
Anaemia	Reduction in red blood cells which can make the skin pale and cause weakness or breathlessness.
Leucopenia	Reduction in the number of white blood cells, which makes infections more likely.
Aspartate aminotransferase increased, alanine aminotransferase increased, LFT increased	Blood tests which show changes in the way the liver is working.
Anaphylactic, anaphylactoid reaction	Serious allergic reaction which causes difficulty in breathing or dizziness.
Angina pectoris	Chest pain.
Angioedema, angioneurotic oedema	Serious allergic reaction which causes swelling of the face or throat.
Aplastic anaemia	Severe reduction in blood cells which can cause weakness, bruising or make infections more likely.
Arrhythmia	Irregular heart beat.

Ataxia	Difficulty in controlling movements.
Bradycardia	Slower heart beat.
Bronchoconstriction, bronchospasm	Difficulty in breathing or wheezing.
Cardiac failure/heart failure	Heart problems which can cause shortness of breath or ankle swelling.
Cerebrovascular accident	Stroke.
Colitis	Inflammation which causes abdominal pain or diarrhoea.
Deep vein thrombosis/venous thromboembolism (VTE)	Blood clot, usually in a leg, which causes pain, swelling or redness.
Dyspepsia	Indigestion.
Ectopic pregnancy	Pregnancy outside the womb which can cause severe pain, bleeding or collapse.
Electrocardiogram QT prolonged	Abnormal ECG heart tracing.
Emotional lability	Mood swings.
Haemolytic anaemia	Reduction in red blood cells which can make the skin pale or yellow and cause weakness or breathlessness.
Hypo/hyperkalaemia	Hypokalaemia: Low blood levels of potassium which can cause muscle weakness, twitching or abnormal heart rhythm. Hyperkalaemia: High blood levels of potassium which can cause abnormal heart rhythm.
Hypo/hypernatraemia	Hyponatraemia: Low blood levels of sodium which can cause tiredness and confusion, muscle twitching, fits or coma. Hypernatraemia: High blood levels of sodium which can cause confusion, muscle twitching or abnormal heart rhythm.
Hypomania	Feeling over-excited.

124

Hypo/hyperthyroidism	Hypothyroidism: Underactive thyroid gland which can cause tiredness or weight gain. Hyperthyroidism: Overactive thyroid gland which can cause increased appetite, weight loss or sweating.
Insomnia	Difficulty in sleeping.
Jaundice	Yellowing of the skin or whites of the eyes caused by liver or blood problems.
Mania	Feeling elated or over-excited, which causes unusual behaviour.
Myocardial infarction	Heart attack.
Myopathy	Pain or weakness in muscles.
Nephritis	Inflammation of the kidney which can cause swollen ankles or high blood pressure.
Orthostatic hypotension/postural hypotension	A fall in blood pressure on standing up which causes dizziness, light-headedness or fainting.
Pancreatitis	Inflammation of the pancreas, which causes severe pain in the abdomen and back.
Pancytopenia	Severe reduction in blood cells which can cause weakness, bruising or make infections more likely.
Paraesthesia of extremities	Tingling or numbness in the hands and feet.
Parkinsonism	Tremor, stiffness and shuffling.
Periorbital oedema	Swelling around the eyes.
Peripheral neuropathy	A disorder of the nerves which can cause weakness, tingling or numbness.
Pneumonitis	Inflammation of the lungs which causes breathlessness, cough and raised temperature.
Prostatism	An enlarged prostate gland which causes difficulty in passing urine in men.
Pulmonary embolism	Blood clot in the lungs which causes chest pain and breathlessness.

Pulmonary fibrosis	Scarring of the lungs which causes shortness of breath.
Raynaud's phenomenon	Poor blood circulation which makes the toes and fingers numb and pale.
Rhabdomyolysis	Abnormal muscle breakdown which can lead to kidney problems.
Stevens–Johnson syndrome	Serious illness with blistering of the skin, mouth, eyes and genitals.
Systemic lupus erythematosus	Allergic condition which causes joint pain, skin rashes and fever.
Tachycardia	Faster heart beat.
Tardive dyskinesia	Uncontrollable movements of mouth, tongue and limbs.
Thrombocytopenia	Reduction in blood platelets, which increases risk of bleeding or bruising.
Torsades de pointes (also ventricular arrhythmias)	Life-threatening irregular heart beat.
Toxic epidermal necrolysis	Serious illness with blistering of the skin.
Uveitis	Inflammation of the eye which causes pain and redness.
Vasculitis	Inflammation of blood vessels, often with skin rash.
Ventricular fibrillation	Life-threatening irregular heart beat.
Vertigo	A feeling of dizziness or "spinning".

Principles for developing definitions:

1. How to use these definitions: the wording of each leaflet should be considered individually to ensure that the specific information for that medicine is conveyed accurately and in a way that is comprehensible to most of the intended readers. User testing will help to identify if there are specific problems in comprehension or interpretation. This should focus in particular on any areas where the patient has to take action if an adverse effect is suspected.

2. When to use lay definitions: definitions should be used when the medical term is not well known in the general population.

3. Level of detail: it will be appropriate to include more details to enable the reader to identify possible symptoms of an adverse effect where this is a key safety issue and the patient should take action to prevent further harm. It may be appropriate to group effects into broad categories such as "heart problems" and provide a lesser degree of detail for very rare and minor effects where specific instructions on action are not needed.

4. General format: the standard format is to describe what the condition is and then what a sufferer may feel. This latter is to help patients in identifying whether they may be suffering from the effect described. This may not be necessary if the condition is well known or the symptoms obvious from the description of the condition.

5. Inclusion of medical terms: pharmaceutical companies should also consider including the medical term where this is an important feature and may help the reader interpret other sources of information about the medicine.

6. Where to use these definitions: these definitions should be used to describe adverse effects of the medication. They may also be used in other sections such as warnings but may not be necessary. For example, a patient suffering from myasthenia gravis would usually recognise the name of the condition. However, a brief description of the type of condition may be helpful to other users.

7. Alternative wordings: there may be circumstances where alternative wording is considered more appropriate, in which case justification should be provided.

8. Serious: use this term to indicate that the condition is usually medically significant (eg is likely to require medical attention, such as hospitalisation). For example, Stevens-Johnson syndrome causes serious blistering and anaphylaxis is a serious allergic reaction. This is not necessary when the seriousness of the condition is obvious or well known.

9. Severe: where necessary to distinguish from symptoms or medical effects that might otherwise be considered as mild (eg severe headache, or severe pain accompanying myocardial infarction).

10. Life-threatening: this should be used very rarely and where this is not obvious. The term should be reserved for a condition that of itself is usually fatal if untreated (in more than 50% of cases).

11. Brackets: use these for the medical term where it is helpful to quote this.

12. "Quote marks": use rarely when needed to distinguish colloquial descriptive terms not to be taken literally, such as feeling "high", from other terms.

MHRA
May 2005

ANNEX 9

REPORT OF PILOT TESTING OF A LEAFLET ON THE RISKS AND BENEFITS OF MEDICINES

CONTENTS:

Final leaflet text in question and answer format

Final leaflet in factsheet format

Issues and questions asked in pilot testing

Response sheet

Review of responses

Tested leaflet text in question and answer format

Tested leaflet in factsheet format

MHRA
January 2005

Side effects of medicine – some questions and answers

What is this leaflet about?

This leaflet aims to answer some questions you may have about taking medicines and the risk of side effects. You will find more information about your particular medicine in the patient information leaflet provided with your medicine. If you have not received a leaflet, please ask your pharmacist to get one for you.

Need further advice?

If you need further advice about medicines remember you can ask your doctor or pharmacist or call NHS Direct & NHS Wales/Galw Iechyd Cymru on 0845 46 47 (text phone 0845 606 46 47) or NHS 24 (Scotland) on 08454 24 24 (textphone 18001 08454 24 24).

1. How do medicines work?

There are a number of ways in which medicines work. The medicine you are taking may:

- **cure your condition,** for example an antibiotic to treat an infection;
- **control your condition,** for example a medicine to lower blood pressure;
- **treat the symptoms of your condition,** for example a painkiller to take for toothache;
- **to prevent you from becoming unwell,** for example a vaccine.

2. Will my medicine cause side effects?

- The expected benefit of your medicine will generally be greater than the risk of you suffering any harmful side effects.
- All medicines can cause problems but most people do not experience serious side effects.
- Your patient information leaflet will list all the known side effects associated with your medicine.

> **Remember: most people take medicines without suffering any side effects.**

3. What is meant by a "common" or "rare" side effect?

The chance, or risk, of having a side effect can be described using words or figures or both. This is how risk may be described in your patient information leaflet:

- Very common means that more than 1 in 10 people taking the medicine are likely to have the side effect.
- Common means that between 1 in 10 and 1 in 100 people are affected
- Uncommon means that between 1 in 100 and 1 in 1,000 people are affected
- Rare means that between 1 in 1,000 and 1 in 10,000 people are affected
- Very rare means that fewer than 1 in 10,000 people are affected

> **Remember: if a side effect has a risk of 1 in 10,000, then 9,999 out of every 10,000 people taking the medicine are not expected to experience that side effect.**

4. Does a high dose increase the risk of side effects?

To get the maximum benefit from your medicine you need to take the recommended dose for you.

- For medicines you have bought yourself, this can be found on the carton or container label and in the patient information leaflet.
- For medicines that have been prescribed by your doctor, the correct dosage will be on the pharmacy label. It is important to remember that the doctor will have prescribed a dose for you that takes into account your age, weight, how ill you are and any other medicines you may be taking. Only change your dose if you have discussed it with your doctor first.
- For some medicines, you will start on a low dose that will gradually be increased over a period of weeks or months, whereas for other medicines you will remain on the same dose throughout your course of treatment.

Sometimes, when you need to stop taking a medicine, your doctor will gradually decrease the dose to avoid unpleasant withdrawal effects. You should not increase or decrease the dose prescribed by your doctor unless you have discussed it with him/her first.

In general, a high dose of a medicine is more likely to cause side effects. However, high doses are sometimes needed to ensure maximum benefit. If you feel unwell after your dose has been increased, remember to check the patient information leaflet or speak to your doctor or pharmacist.

5. How can I reduce the risk of side effects?

- Take your medicine as your doctor or pharmacist has advised you.
- Be careful about mixing medicines. Some medicines should not be taken together. Before taking a new medicine, it is important to tell your doctor or pharmacist about any other medicines you are already taking, including herbal remedies or any non-prescription medicines you may have bought for yourself in a pharmacy or supermarket

- Understand about "risk factors". Sometimes "risk factors" increase the chance of your medicine causing side effects. These factors will vary depending on what medicine you are taking. You may be able to lower your risk of side effects by avoiding these factors, for example by not drinking alcohol or eating certain foods during your course of treatment. Your patient information leaflet will tell you about any known risk and what you can do to reduce the chance of side effects.

6. Do side effects always occur immediately?

- Some side effects can happen immediately (for example an allergic reaction).
- Others might not start for several days or weeks (for example skin rashes) or even longer (for example stomach problems with some painkillers).
- In general, side effects are most likely to when you start a new medicine or after your dose has been increased.
- Quite often, mild side effects will go away as your body adjusts to the new medicine or dose.

7 What should I do if I feel unwell after taking my medicine?

- Your patient information leaflet may contain all the advice you need. If you are in doubt, speak to your doctor, nurse or pharmacist or call NHS Direct, NHS Direct Wales/Galw Iechyd Cymru or NHS 24 on the numbers given at the beginning of this factsheet.
- For worrying or serious symptoms you may have to stop taking the medicine, or need other treatment.
- For less serious side effects, you may be advised to continue with your medicine, or change the dose.

8. Will my medicine affect my lifestyle?

Although most medicines will not affect your lifestyle, some can. Examples of how some side effects can affect the way you live are listed below:

- Some medicines may affect your vision or co-ordination or make you sleepy. This may affect your ability to drive, ride a bicycle or perform skilled tasks safely.
- Some medicines may affect your sex drive.
- You may need to avoid drinking alcohol or eating certain foods while taking some medicines.

Remember: your patient information leaflet will tell you about any lifestyle issues and advise you about things you should avoid.

131

Further Information on Benefits and Side Effects for Patients Taking Medicines

This factsheet provides some additional information on taking medicines and their side effects. It is intended for you to read alongside the patient information leaflet that you will have received with your medicine. If you have not received a leaflet with your medicine, please ask your pharmacist to get one for you

Other sources of information on medicines: Ask your doctor or pharmacist for advice or call NHS Direct & NHS Wales/Galw Iechyd Cymru on 0845 46 47 (text phone 0845 606 46 47) or NHS 24 (Scotland) on 08454 24 24 (textphone 18001 08454 24 24).

1. Some ways medicines work

There are a number of ways in which medicines work. The medicine you are taking may:

■ **cure your condition,** for example an antibiotic to treat an infection;

■ **control your condition,** for example a medicine to lower blood pressure;

■ **treat the symptoms of your condition,** for example a painkiller to take for toothache;

■ **to prevent you from becoming unwell,** for example a vaccine.

2. Side effects: some advice on the risks and how you may be able to reduce them

Risk of side effects

The expected benefit of your medicine will generally be greater than the risk of you suffering any harmful side effects. All medicines can cause problems and your patient information leaflet will list all the known side effects associated with your medicine. However, it is important to note that most people take medicines without suffering any side effects.

The chance of suffering from a side effect can be described using words or figures or both. The following information shows how risk may be described in your leaflet:

Very common means that **more than 1 in 10** people taking the medicine are likely to have the side effect.

Common means that **between 1 in 10 and 1 in 100** people are affected

Uncommon means that **between 1 in 100 and 1 in 1,000** people are affected

Rare means that **between 1 in 1,000 and 1 in 10,000** people are affected

Very rare means that **fewer than 1 in 10,000** people are affected

Remember: if a side effect is said to have a risk of 1 in 10,000, then 9,999 out of every 10,000 people taking the medicine are not expected to experience that side effect.

Dosage and the risk of side effects

To get the maximum benefit from your medicine you need to take the recommended dose. For medicines you have bought yourself, this can be found on the carton or container label and in the patient information leaflet. For medicines that have been prescribed by your doctor, the correct dosage will be on the pharmacy label. It is important to remember that the doctor will prescribe a dose for you that takes into account your age, weight, illness and any other medicines you may be taking. Only change your dose if you have discussed it with your doctor first.

For some medicines, you may start on a low dose and be advised to gradually increase this over a period of weeks or months, whereas for other medicines you may remain on the same dose throughout your course of treatment. In general, a high dose of a medicine is more likely to cause side effects. However, in some cases this will be the dose that will also give you the greatest benefit. If you feel unwell after your dose has been increased, remember to check the patient information leaflet or speak to your doctor or pharmacist. Sometimes, when you need to stop taking a medicine, your doctor will gradually decrease the dose to avoid unpleasant withdrawal effects. You should not increase or decrease the dose prescribed by your doctor unless you have discussed it with him/her first.

Reducing the risk of side effects

Some medicines should not be taken together. Before taking a new medicine, it is important to tell your doctor or pharmacist about any other medicines you are taking. This includes herbal remedies and medicines you may have bought for yourself in a pharmacy or supermarket.

There may be "risk factors" that will increase the chance of your medicine causing side effects. You may be able to lower your risk of side effects by avoiding these factors, for example by not drinking alcohol or eating certain foods during your course of treatment. Your patient information leaflet will give advice about factors that may increase the risk of you experiencing side effects with your medicine and action that you can take to reduce these risks.

3. When to look out for side effects

Some side effects may affect you immediately after starting a medicine, for example an allergic reaction. You may not notice other side effects for several days or weeks, for example skin rashes. In some cases it may be much longer, for example stomach problems with some painkillers. In general, side effects tend to occur shortly after starting a new medicine or after your dose has been increased. Quite often mild side effects will go away as your body adjusts to the new medicine or dose.

4. What to do if you think your medicine has caused side effects

If you think your medicine is making you feel unwell, check the patient information leaflet as it may contain all the advice you need. If you are still unsure what to do, speak to your doctor, nurse or pharmacist or call NHS Direct, NHS Direct Wales/Galw Iechyd Cymru or NHS 24 on the numbers given at the beginning of this factsheet.

5. Lifestyle

Many medicines will not affect your lifestyle or day to day activities but some can. Some medicines may affect your ability to drive or operate machinery, your sex drive or whether you should drink alcohol or eat certain foods. Your patient information leaflet will provide advice on these issues.

Issues and Questions

Key Issue	Question
Users need to know why these leaflets have been produced and what they're for	Looking at this leaflet, is it clear what it's meant to be used for?
Users should know that there are other sources of information available	Does this leaflet suggest anywhere else you might go to find out about medicines?
Users should understand that medicines work in different ways	From what you see here, can you give any examples of different ways medicines might work?
People should believe that licensed medicines are more likely to do good than harm	From what you've read here, which would you say is more likely: side effects or benefits from a medicine?
People should be able to make realistic estimates of the likelihood of side effects, based on the definitions offered here	OK, based on this leaflet, if a medicine has a rare side effect – how likely is it that you'll get this?
We'd like people to understand that side effects are usually dose related	Does a high dose increase the risk of side effects?
We want people to know how they can reduce their risks of side effects	Can you tell me a couple of ways to lower your risk of side effects?
People need to understand when side effects are likely to happen	In general, when are side effects most likely to happen?
We'd like readers to be aware of the risks of mixing medicines	Is there any advice here about one medicine affecting another? What does it say?
People need to know what to do if they do get a side effect	Let's say you were taking a medicine and thought you were suffering a side effect. What does this leaflet tell you to do?
We would like people to understand about risk factors and side effects	Is there anything in the leaflet about what you eat and drink and how that may affect medicines?
We want people to understand that there are medicines that interfere with lifestyle	Do you see any examples of ways in which medicines can interfere with the way you live? What are they?

Questions to be asked

1. Let's say you were taking a medicine and thought you were suffering a side effect. What does this leaflet tell you to do?

2. Can you tell me a couple of ways to lower your risk of side effects?

3. Does this leaflet suggest anywhere else you might go to find out about medicines?

4. Does a high dose increase the risk of side effects?

5. Do you see any examples of ways in which medicines can interfere with the way you live? What are they?

6. OK, based on this leaflet, if a medicine has a rare side effect – how likely is it that you'll get this?

7. Is there any advice here about one medicine affecting another? What does it say?

8. From what you see here, can you give any examples of different ways medicines might work?

9. In general, when are side effects most likely to happen?

10. From what you've read here, which would you say is more likely: side effects or benefits from a medicine?

11. Looking at this leaflet, is it clear what it's meant to be used for?

12. Is there anything in the leaflet about what you eat and drink and how that may affect medicines?

Response sheet

1. Check the PIL ☐
   Check with hcp ☐
   Call NHSD/NHS24 ☐
   Other (tester to note)

   Information located : quickly ☐
   with difficulty ☐
   not located ☐

2. Take medicines as directed by hcp ☐
   Care with mixing medicines ☐
   (tell hcp about other meds/herbals)
   Read PIL to check for risk factors ☐
   Low start dose ☐
   Reduce dose gradually ☐
   Other (tester to note)

   Information located : quickly ☐
   with difficulty ☐
   not located ☐

3. Doctor ☐
   Pharmacist ☐
   NHSD/NHS24 ☐
   Other (tester to note)

   Information located : quickly ☐
   with difficulty ☐
   not located ☐

4. More likely to lead to side effects ☐
   Other (tester to note))

   Information located : quickly ☐
   with difficulty ☐
   not located ☐

5. Feeling sleepy   ☐
    (driving/skilled tasks)
    Sex drive   ☐
    Food/drink   ☐
    Other (tester to note)

Information located :   quickly   ☐
    with difficulty   ☐
    not located   ☐

6. Between 1 in 1,000 and 1 in 10,000   ☐
    Other (tester to note)

Information located :   quickly   ☐
    with difficulty   ☐
    not located   ☐

7. Care with mixing medicines   ☐
    Tell hcp about other meds or   ☐
    herbals already taking
       Other (tester to note)

Information located :   quickly   ☐
    with difficulty   ☐
    not located   ☐

8. Cure   ☐
    Control   ☐
    Treat   ☐
    Prevent   ☐
    Other (tester to note)

Information located :   quickly   ☐
    with difficulty   ☐
    not located   ☐

9. After starting a new medicine   ☐
    After a dose increase   ☐
    Other (tester to note)

Information located :   quickly   ☐

            with difficulty ☐

            not located ☐

10. Medicines more likely to benefit ☐

   Agree?   Yes ☐   No ☐

Information located :   quickly   ☐

            with difficulty ☐

            not located ☐

11. To read alongside PIL provided ☐

   Other (tester to note)

Information located :   quickly   ☐

            with difficulty ☐

            not located ☐

12. Foods   ☐

   Alcohol   ☐

   Check PIL   ☐

   Other (tester to note)

Information located :   quickly   ☐

            with difficulty ☐

            not located ☐

13. Score for usefulness of leaflet 1 (not useful at all) to 5 (very useful)

14. Score for usefulness of alternative format leaflet 1 (not useful at all) to 5 (very useful)

Name of volunteer:

Age:

Date / Time of test: Voucher received:

QUESTION	1	2	3	4	5	6	7	8	9	10	11	12	M/F	AGE	FORMAT	SCORE out of 5	ALT SCORE out of 5	PREF FORMAT
TEST 1	✓	X	✓	X (NL)	✓	✓	X (NL)	✓	X (NL)	✓	✓	✓	F	59	FACT	4	4	Q/A
TEST 2	✓	✓	✓	✓	✓	✓	✓	✓	✓	✓	✓	✓	F	23	Q/A	4	3	Q/A
TEST 3	✓ (WD)	✓	✓	✓ (WD)	✓	✓	✓	✓	X (NL)	X	✓	✓	F	53	Q/A	3-3.5	4	Q/A
TEST 4	✓ (WD)	✓	✓	✓	✓	✓	✓	✓	✓	✓	✓	✓	M	24	Q/A	4	3.5	Q/A
TEST 5	✓	✓	✓	✓	✓	✓	✓	✓	✓	✓	✓	✓	F	30	FACT	4.5	3.5-4	FACT
TEST 6	✓	✓	✓	X	✓	✓	✓	✓	✓	✓	✓	✓	M	33	FACT	3.5-4	3.5-4	Q/A
TEST 7	✓	✓	✓	✓	✓	✓	✓	✓	✓	✓	✓	✓	F	58	FACT	4	3	FACT
TEST 8	✓	✓ (WD)	✓	✓ (WD)	✓	X (NL)	✓	✓	X (NL)	✓	✓	✓	M	52	FACT	5	5	QA
TEST 9	✓	✓	✓	X (NL)	✓	✓	✓	✓	✓	✓	✓	✓	M	51	Q/A	4	3	Q/A
TEST 10	✓	✓	✓	X (NL)	✓	✓	✓	✓	✓	✓	✓	✓	F	29	Q/A	5	2	Q/A
TOTAL CORRECT	10	9	10	6	10	10	8	10	7	9	10	10						Q/A (av score **3.9-4.05** vs **3.65-3.7** for factsheet)

Key: ✓: correct answer
X: incorrect answer
WD: information located with difficulty
NL: information not located

139

QA positive comments	QA negative comments	Factsheet positive comments	Factsheet negative comments
Easier to read (#1, #4, #6)	Other sources of information (NHS Direct etc) repeated unnecessarily (#3)	Like boxes around information (particularly other sources of information) (#2, #4, #6, #7)	Other sources of information (NHS Direct etc) repeated unnecessarily (#3)
Like bullet points (#2)	Panel with numbers not necessary(#3, #6, #8)		Panel with numbers not necessary (#3, #6, #8)
Lifestyle info useful (#6, #9)	Importance of PIL needs to be highlighted (#3, #4, #5, #7)		Headings for cure/control/treat and very common/common etc should be made to stand out more (#4)
Very clear layout (#6, #9)			Importance of PIL needs to be highlighted (#3, #4, #5 #7)
Definition of rare/common etc is very useful (#9)			Benefit vs risk statement is scary (#8)
Useful format for patients not familiar with taking medicines/ reading medical documents (#10)	Could be improved with pictures (egcartoon type drawing of someone reading a leaflet etc..)(#10)		Not easy to read (#2, #4)

Positive and negative feedback raised by individuals during the user testing procedure has been summarized in the above table. The figure presented in parentheses represents the number of people raising a specific issue.

Formatting changes, which were raised by most participants, have been incorporated into the documents. These were:

- addition of bullet points (factsheet only)
- placing important information in rectangles (Q/A and factsheet)
- emboldening important information (Q/A and factsheet)

Question & Response	Comments & Answers Given	Amendments made to leaflets
1. **Let's say you were taking a medicine and thought you were suffering a side effect. What does this leaflet tell you to do?** *Check PIL;check with hcp;call NHSD/NHS24*	▪ located and gave correct answer. Additional comment "Depends on symptoms" (#4) ▪ identified correct section – gave correct answer plus "stop taking the tablets" (100)	Added information in this section about patient reporting (yellow cards) following launch of this initiative
2. **Can you tell me a couple of ways to lower the risk of side effects?** *Care with mixing medicines (tell hcp about other meds/herbals; read PIL to check risk factors; low start dose; reduce dose gradually*	▪ talk to hcp (located in section 4). As this was not correct section no other examples given (#1) ▪ identified correct section – gave first three as examples (#2) ▪ identified correct section – gave first two as examples (#3) ▪ identified correct section – gave first two examples plus food and alcohol (#4, #8) ▪ identified correct section – gave correct answer plus food and alcohol (#6, #9) ▪ identified correct section – gave first two as examples (#7) ▪ identified correct section – gave correct answer plus alcohol (#10)	Because question asked for a "couple" of ways, often only the first two ways listed in the relevant section were given. The PIL was not often mentioned. Taking this alongside comments to Q11, reference to the PIL has been highlighted in the beginning, middle and end of the leaflet.
3. **Does this leaflet suggest anywhere else you may go to find out about medicines?** *Doctor; pharmacist; NHSD/NHS24.*	▪ this information is repeated unnecessarily in leaflet (#3) located and gave correct answer; additional answer – PIL (#5, #10)	

Question & Response	Comments & Answers Given	Amendments made to leaflets
4. Does a high dose increase the risk of side effects? *More likely to lead to side effects*	■ you should take recommended dose, prescribed by the doctor (#1) ■ located and gave correct answer. Commented this statement was scary (#2) ■ you should take according to PIL/label. Correct answer identified after reading relevant section right through again (#3) ■ no. You should take the dose suggested (#6, #9, #10) ■ located (with difficulty) and gave correct answer. Commented this question/answer was confusing because of the advice about starting medicines with a high dose and gradually reducing it. Why give a dose that will give side effects? (#8)	This question caused the most difficulty with participants. This section of the leaflet has been rearranged to state that a high dose is more likely to give you side effects. However this could lead to patients reducing the dose or not taking the medicine and further rearrangement of this section may be required.
5. Do you see any examples of ways in which medicines can interfere with the way you live? What are they? *Feeling sleepy (driving/skilled tasks); sex drive; food/drink.*		
6. OK, based on this leaflet, if a medicine has a rare side effect – how likely is it that you will get this? *Between 1 in 1000 and 1 in 10 000*	■ located and gave correct answer. Unsure whether these figures would apply to all medicines (#2) ■ additional comment – good to explain figures positively (positive framing statement) (#5) ■ located and gave correct answer. Commented that they did not understand the figures and the definitions did not meet their understanding of "odds". Rare does not mean this to a betting person (#8) ■ thought this section explained the terms "rare" etc very well (#9)	General comment indicated this information would be better contained in a box so that patients could either focus on it or ignore a self-contained piece of information they found difficult to understand. The positive framing appeared helpful and this was brought into the box and emboldened.

Question & Response	Comments & Answers Given	Amendments made to leaflets
7 Is there any advice here about one medicine affecting another. What does it say? *Care with mixing medicines; tell hcp about other meds/herbals already taking.*	■ can't find any information about this (#1, #8) ■ additional comment: supermarket medicines might be helpful (#5, #6)	
8. From what you see here , can you give any examples of different ways medicines might work? *Cure; control; treat; prevent.*		
9. In general, when are side effects most likely to happen? *After starting a new medicine; after a dose increase.*	■ if you do things you are not supposed to do liking mixing medicines (#1) ■ when the side effect is more common. Correct answer not located (#3) ■ located and gave correct answer also mention changes to other medicines patient may be taking (#4) ■ could not find this information. When correct location was pointed at (at request of participant) admitted that they had read this section and still missed it (#8) ■ identified correct section – gave correct answer plus information on immediate effects, delayed effects (#10)	Moved to the beginning of section 3 (_new change)
10. From what you've read here, which would you say is more likely: side effects or benefits from a medicine? *Medicine more likely to benefit.*	■ located and gave correct answer. Commented this section was not particularly clear and that "harmful" side effects is a scary statement (#2) ■ side effects are more likely (#3) ■ located and gave correct answer. Commented that overall impression of leaflet was about side effects – benefits not obvious (#5)	Added benefit to the title of the QA leaflet (_new change) Rearranged the bullet points at the start of section to concentrate on benefits (_new change) Consider replacing "harmful" – unpleasant??

143

Question & Response	Comments & Answers Given	Amendments made to leaflets
11. Looking at the leaflet is it clear what its meant to be used for? *To read alongside the PIL provided*	■ correctly described use of leaflet but commented the importance of PIL needed to be more obvious (#2, #7) ■ correctly described use of leaflet; commented it may make patient more aware of side effects (#4) ■ thought the use of the leaflet alongside PIL was very clear (#9)	See Q2 above
12. Is there anything in the leaflet about what you eat and drink and how that may affect medicines? *Foods; alcohol; check PIL.*	■ showed where this information can be found in two locations – correct answer given (#5)	

Further information on benefits and side effects for patients taking medicines

This factsheet provides some additional information on taking medicines and the risk of side effects. You will find more information about your particular medicine in the **patient information leaflet** provided with your medicine.

If you have received a medicine but no leaflet, please ask your pharmacist to get one for you.

Other sources of information on medicines: If you need further advice about medicines remember you can ask your doctor or pharmacist or call NHS Direct & NHS Wales/Galw Iechyd Cymru on 0845 46 47 (text phone 0845 606 46 47) or NHS 24 (Scotland) on 08454 24 24 (textphone 18001 08454 24 24).

1. Some ways medicines work

The medicine you are taking may:

■ **cure your condition**, for example an antibiotic, which is used to treat an infection.

■ **control your condition** - for example a medicine to lower your blood pressure.

■ **treat the symptoms of your condition** - for example a painkiller to take for toothache.

■ **prevent you from becoming unwell** - for example a vaccination against disease.

2. Side effects: some advice on the risks and how you may be able to reduce them

Risk of side effects

■ The expected benefit of your medicine will usually be greater than the risk of you suffering any harmful side effects.

■ Most people take medicines without suffering any side effects.

■ However, all medicines can cause problems and your patient information leaflet will list all the known side effects linked to your medicine.

The chance (the risk) of having a side effect can be described using words or figures or both. This is how risk may be described in your patient information leaflet:

Very common means that more than 1 in 10 people taking the medicine are likely to have the side effect.

Common means that between 1 in 10 and 1 in 100 people are affected

Uncommon means that between 1 in 100 and 1 in 1,000 people are affected

Rare means that between 1 in 1,000 and 1 in 10,000 people are affected

Very rare means that fewer than 1 in 10,000 people are affected

Remember if a side effect is said to have a risk of 1 in 10,000, then 9,999 out of every 10,000 people taking the medicine are not expected to experience that side effect.

Dosage and the risk of side effects

In general, a high dose of a medicine is more likely to cause side effects. However, high doses are sometimes needed to ensure maximum benefit.

To get the maximum benefit from your medicine you need to take the recommended dose for you.

■ For medicines you have bought yourself, the dose is written on the carton or container label and in the patient information leaflet.

■ For medicines that have been prescribed by your doctor, the dose will be on the pharmacy label. The doctor will have prescribed a dose for you that takes into account your age, weight, illness and any other medicines you may be taking. Only change your dose if you have discussed it with your doctor first.

■ With some medicines, you may start on a low dose that will gradually be increased over weeks (or months). With other medicines you will stay on the same dose throughout your course of treatment.

■ Sometimes, when you need to stop taking a medicine, your doctor will gradually reduce the dose to avoid unpleasant withdrawal effects. You should not increase or decrease the dose prescribed by your doctor unless you have discussed it with him/her first.

Reducing the risk of side effects

- Take your medicine as your doctor or pharmacist has advised you.

- Be careful about mixing medicines. Some medicines should not be taken together. Before taking a new medicine, it is important to tell your doctor or pharmacist about any other medicines you are taking, including herbal remedies or any non-prescription medicines you may have bought for yourself in a pharmacy or supermarket.

- Understand about "risk factors". Sometimes risk factors increase the chance of your medicine causing side effects. These factors will vary depending on what medicine you are taking. These factors will vary depending on what medicine you are taking. For example, you may be able to lower your risk of side effects by not drinking alcohol or not eating certain foods during your course of treatment. Your patient information leaflet will tell you about any known risk and what you can do to reduce the chance of side effects.

3. When to look out for side effects

When side effects happen depends on the medicine and the person taking it.

- Some side effects happen immediately – for example an allergic reaction.

- Others might not start for several days or weeks – for example skin rashes – or even longer – for example stomach problems with some painkillers.

- In general, side effects tend to occur shortly after starting a new medicine or after your dose has been increased.

- Quite often mild side effects will go away as your body adjusts to the new medicine or dose.

4. What to do if you think your medicine has caused side effects

- Check the patient information leaflet: it may contain all the advice you need.

- If in doubt, speak to your doctor, nurse or pharmacist or call NHS Direct, NHS Direct Wales/Galw Iechyd Cymru or NHS 24 on the numbers given at the beginning of this factsheet.

- For worrying or serious side effects, you may have to stop taking the medicine, or need other treatment.

- For less serious side effects, you may be advised to continue with your medicine or change the dose.

- You or your health adviser can report suspected side effects to the drug safety watchdog (MHRA). Telephone 020 7084 2000 to find out moe.

5. Lifestyle

Many medicines will not affect your lifestyle or day to day activities but some can. Some medicines may affect your ability to drive or operate machinery, your sex drive or whether you should drink alcohol or eat certain foods.

Your patient information leaflet will provide advice on lifestyle issues and things you should avoid whilst taking your medicine.

Benefits and side effects of medicines – some questions and answers

What is this leaflet about?

This leaflet aims to answer some questions you may have about taking medicines and the risk of side effects. You will find more information about your particular medicine in **the patient information leaflet** provided with your medicine.

If you have received a medicine but no leaflet, please ask your pharmacist to get one for you.

Need further advice?

If you need further advice about medicines remember you can ask your doctor or pharmacist or call NHS Direct & NHS Wales/Galw Iechyd Cymru on 0845 46 47 (text phone 0845 606 46 47) or NHS 24 (Scotland) on 08454 24 24 (textphone 18001 08454 24 24).

1. How do medicines work?

The medicine you are taking may:

- **cure your condition** – for example an antibiotic, which is used to treat an infection;

- **control your condition** – for example a medicine to lower your blood pressure;

- **treat the symptoms of your condition** – for example a painkiller to take for toothache;

- **prevent you from becoming unwell**, for example a vaccination against disease.

2. Will my medicine cause side effects?

- The expected benefit of your medicine will usually be greater than the risk of suffering any harmful side effects.

- Most people take medicines without suffering any side effects.

- However, all medicines can cause problems. Your patient information leaflet will list all the known side effects linked to your medicine.

Important: most people take medicines without suffering any side effects.

3. What is meant by a "common" or "rare" side effect?

The chance (the risk) of having a side effect can be described using words or figures or both. This is how risk may be described in your patient information leaflet:

- **Very common** means that more than 1 in 10 people taking the medicine are likely to have the side effect.

- **Common** means that between 1 in 10 and 1 in 100 people are affected

- **Uncommon** means that between 1 in 100 and 1 in 1,000 people are affected

- **Rare** means that between 1 in 1,000 and 1 in 10,000 people are affected

- **Very rare** means that fewer than 1 in 10,000 people are affected

Remember if a side effect has a risk of 1 in 10,000, then 9,999 out of every 10,000 people taking the medicine are not expected to experience that side effect.

4. Does a high dose increase the risk of side effects?

In general, a high dose of a medicine is more likely to cause side effects.

However, high doses are sometimes needed to ensure maximum benefit.

To get the maximum benefit from your medicine you need to take the recommended dose for you.

- For medicines you have bought yourself, the dose is written on the carton or container label and in the patient information leaflet.

- For medicines that have been prescribed by your doctor, the dose will be on the pharmacy label. The doctor will have prescribed a dose for you that takes into account your age, weight, how ill you are and any other medicines you may be taking. Only change your dose if you have discussed it with your doctor first.

- With some medicines, you will start on a low dose that will gradually be increased over a period of weeks (or months). With other medicines you will stay on the same dose throughout your course of treatment.

- Sometimes, when you need to stop taking a medicine, your doctor will gradually reduce the dose to avoid unpleasant withdrawal effects. You should not increase or decrease the dose prescribed by your doctor unless you have discussed it with him/her first.

Important: check the patient information leaflet and speak to your doctor or pharmacist if you feel unwell after your dose has been increased.

5. How can I reduce the risk of side effects?

- Take your medicine as your doctor or pharmacist has advised you.
- Be careful about mixing medicines. Some medicines should not be taken together. Before taking a new medicine, it is important to tell your doctor or pharmacist about any other medicines you are already taking, including herbal remedies or any non-prescription medicines you may have bought for yourself in a pharmacy or supermarket.
- Understand about "risk factors". Sometimes risk factors increase the

chance of your medicine causing side effects. These factors will vary depending on what medicine you are taking. For example, you may be able to lower your risk of side effects by not drinking alcohol or not eating certain foods during your course of treatment. Your patient information leaflet will tell you about any known risk and what you can do to reduce the chance of side effects.

6. Do side effects always come on straight away?

- It depends on the medicine and the person.
- Some side effects can happen immediately – for example an allergic reaction
- Others might not start for several days or weeks – for example skin rashes – or even longer – for example stomach problems with some painkillers
- In general, side effects are most likely to when you start a new medicine or after your dose has been increased.
- Quite often, mild side effects will go away as your body adjusts to the new medicine or dose.

- Some medicines may affect your sex drive.
- You may need to stop drinking alcohol or eating certain foods while taking some medicines.

Important: your patient information leaflet will tell you about any lifestyle issues and advise you about things you should avoid.

7. What should I do if I feel unwell after taking my medicine?

- Check your patient information leaflet: it may contain all the advice you need.
- If in doubt, speak to your doctor, nurse or pharmacist or call NHS Direct, NHS Direct Wales/Galw Iechyd Cymru or NHS 24 on the numbers given at the beginning of this leaflet.
- For worrying or serious effects you may have to stop taking the medicine, or need other treatment.
- For less serious side effects, you may be advised to continue with your medicine, or change the dose.
- You or your health adviser can report suspected side effects to the drug safety watchdog (MHRA). Telephone 020 7084 2000 to find out more.

8. Will my medicine affect my lifestyle?

Although most medicines will not affect your lifestyle, some can. Examples are:
- Some medicines may affect your vision or co-ordination or make you sleepy. This may affect your ability to drive, ride a bicycle or perform skilled tasks safely.

ANNEX 10
GUIDELINE ON COMMUNICATION OF RISKS AND BENEFITS IN PATIENT INFORMATION LEAFLETS

Medicines and Healthcare products Regulatory Agency

Safeguarding public health

Contents

About this document

Headline information

Presenting benefits of medicines

Presenting information about side effects

1. ABOUT THIS DOCUMENT

The importance of patient information

User information that accompanies medicines is a vital supplement to other forms of communications between healthcare professionals and their patients. Existing guidance on the preparation of patient information leaflets (PILs) is largely focused on specific items of information to be included, and the order of inclusion. To date, there is relatively little guidance on how best to present information in order to optimise understanding and support the safe use of medicines. Such qualitative considerations are critical to effective risk communication.

Any misperception or failure to understand the risks of possible adverse drug reactions (ADRs), either qualitatively or quantitatively, can affect a patient's ability to make rational decisions about taking medicines. Likewise, it is also important that patients understand the potential benefits of their medicine. Failure to adhere to advice or agreement about medication because of exaggerated fears of side effects is one of many possible adverse consequences of misperceptions about risks and potential benefits.

The patient information leaflet has a vital role in providing clear advice for patients on the risk of side effects and what actions to take if they encounter problems when taking their medicines. In particular, patients should know whether to continue taking their medicine and whether (and how urgently) they need to seek medical advice about possible side effects. Careful attention to format and wording is needed to ensure that the information is comprehensive, but not alarmist.

Guidance contained in this document

This document gives guidance on the presentation of patient information leaflets in order to optimise the communication of risk. It has been developed by the MHRA in consultation with the Committee on Safety of Medicines (CSM) Working Group on Patient Information.

It is divided into three sections:

- headline information;

- presenting benefits of medicines;

- presenting information about side effects.

Each section describes principles to be employed when drafting patient information leaflets, together with examples and illustrations to aid interpretation. Although it may not always be possible to apply every principle (for example, due to lack of data), every effort should be made to select the most appropriate principles for each PIL.

User testing is critical to assessing the effectiveness of the presentation of risk information. Therefore, the PIL submission should be accompanied by the results of user testing and an explanation of which of the above principles have/have not been adopted, and justification for any approach which contravenes these principles.

See additional guidance on readability and user testing provided in Annexes 5 and 6

2   HEADLINE INFORMATION

It is known that some patients will not read the patient information leaflet, especially where they perceive it to be too long and/or complex. In an attempt to ensure that patients are aware of key information on the safe and appropriate use of a product, companies are asked to submit proposals for a concise "key information" headline section at the start of the PIL.

Key principles

This section should focus on information that the patient must be aware of in order to ensure safe and effective use of his/her medicine.

General format

i.   **Headline information should be at the beginning of the leaflet**, presented so as to maximise its visibility and the likelihood of it being read. This might include highlighting the text or using a larger font size.

ii.   **Information should be presented as a short series of bullet points.** In most cases between 2 and 6 points should suffice; however, there is no "standard" length, and marketing authorisation holders will need to use their discretion in deciding upon the number and type of headlines. There may be some products for which no headlines would be necessary (for example, simple products for which there are no significant safety issues, such as aqueous cream).

iii. **Only the key messages on safe and appropriate use of the product should be included in this section.** As a general principle, the section should be kept short in order that patients do not rely on it as a substitute for reading the main body of the PIL.

Most suitable types of information for inclusion

iv. Manufacturers should consider which are the most essential messages, bearing in mind the product and its therapeutic context. Typically these may relate to:

- **why the patient should take the product;**

- **the maximum dose or duration of treatment;**

- **potential side effects/withdrawal reactions (symptoms to look out for, especially for common or serious side effects);**

- **contraindications;**

- **important drug interactions;**

- **circumstances in which the drug should be stopped;**

- **what to do if the medicine doesn't work; or**

- **where to find further information.**

v. **"Positive" information on the anticipated benefit of taking the medication should be included** (usually as the first bullet point) in order to provide balance and context for the "negative" information referring to possible adverse events. Positive information should be limited to short factual statements stating the licensed indication (eg "*Your doctor has prescribed [PRODUCT] because it is a treatment for X*). Specific efficacy data or other product claims should <u>not</u> be included.

vi. There should be a standard form of wording indicating **that the patient should read the rest of the leaflet.** The date of the latest revision of the leaflet should be stated, so that long-term users will be aware when there is a need to re-read the PIL.

vii. Consistency across all products containing a particular drug substance and/or drug class is encouraged.

Less suitable types of information

Information on the following types of issues might be less suitable for the headline section:

i. Hypersensitivity (which is almost universally listed as a contraindication) except where it is a significant clinical issue eg penicillin.

ii. Contraindications in uncommon conditions – specifically those which the patient would be expected to be aware of if they have the condition eg porphyria.

iii. Precautions that are primarily relevant for the doctor's decision on whether to prescribe. For example, psychoactive drugs that should be prescribed with caution to patients with a history of drug abuse.

iv. Strict advice to avoid a medicine during pregnancy or lactation should only be included in the headline section if there are important safety data to support this recommendation.

v. Undesirable effects and interactions that represent issues of tolerability rather than of safety (eg gastrointestinal upset, headache), or are unlikely to be of major clinical importance.

vi. Advice relating to rare scenarios in which the patient would seek urgent advice (eg stroke, anaphylaxis, a first seizure) and where the advice in the PIL headline section would be unlikely to have any bearing on the action taken by the patient.

vii. Overdose, unless a particular concern eg paracetamol.

A proposed format with some example headlines

Important things that you need to know about [PRODUCT]:

- Your doctor has prescribed [PRODUCT] because it is a treatment for X.

- If you are pregnant or could get pregnant you should talk to your doctor before taking [PRODUCT].

- Taking some other medicines with [PRODUCT] can cause problems. Tell your doctor if you are taking anything else (including herbal or "natural" remedies). If you are, you should read the section below on "taking other medicines" carefully.

- Do not take more than 4 tablets in 24 hours.

- Do not stop taking this medicine suddenly – you might get a reaction, such as…

- Most people don't get side effects taking [PRODUCT] but some people do – for example inflammation of the liver (hepatitis): see page 2 for more information.

Now read the rest of this leaflet. It includes other important information on the safe and effective use of this medicine that might be especially important for you.

This leaflet was last updated on xx/xx/xx

Some proposed worked examples for the headline section

Example 1 - Carbamazepine 200mg Tablets

Important things that you need to know:

- Carbamazepine tablets are prescribed for different illnesses including epilepsy, manic-depression and neuralgia.

- **Take carbamazepine regularly to get the maximum benefit.** You should not stop taking the medicine without talking to your doctor. Sometimes stopping the medicine can cause problems.

- Carbamazepine can cause side effects, although most people do not have serious problems – see page 2 for details. If you have fever, sore throat, skin rashes or skin yellowing, mouth ulcers, bruising or bleeding, see your doctor immediately.

- Some side effects may occur early in treatment. These often disappear after a few days as your body gets used to the drug (for example dizziness, drowsiness or clumsiness).

- Taking other medicines may sometimes cause problems, including other anti-epilepsy drugs. Check with your doctor or pharmacist before taking any other medicines.

- If you are (or might become) pregnant while taking carbamazepine, it is important to talk to your doctor about this.

Now read the rest of this leaflet. It includes other important information on the safe and effective use of this medicine that might be especially important for you.
This leaflet was last updated on xx/xx/xx

The six bullet points here cover the main safety issues relating to carbamazepine, ie the need to take the medicine regularly for maximum effect, the need to be aware of symptoms of skin, hepatic and blood disorders, potential drug interactions and pregnancy. Informing patients of early side effects that are likely to subside may be important in encouraging compliance. Other important information is not included in this headline section (but is included in the main part of the PIL) as this would reduce the impact of the key messages. Omitted information (with reasons for omission in parentheses) includes:

Contraindications:	Hypersensitivity (this is a standard contraindication)
	History of previous bone marrow depression, or intermittent porphyria or atrioventricular conduction abnormalities (such patients are likely to scrutinise the PIL text and discuss with doctor)
Cautions:	Cardiac, renal or hepatic damage (such patients are likely to scrutinise the PIL text)
	Glaucoma (primarily a prescriber responsibility)
	Photosensitivity (primarily a prescriber responsibility)
Interactions:	Some drugs may raise carbamazepine or decrease serum carbamazepine levels (too numerous for headline use)
Side effects:	Headache, nausea and vomiting and some other side effects (these are relatively minor tolerability issues)

Example 2 - Ciprofloxacin 250mg tablets

Important things that you need to know:

■ Ciprofloxacin is a treatment for some bacterial infections.

■ **Take your tablets regularly until the end of the course – read the label.**

■ Most people do not have serious side effects, but side effects can occur – see page x for details. Some people may feel dizzy or sleepy, especially when they start ciprofloxacin. Drinking alcohol can make these side effects worse. If you feel dizzy or sleepy, it is dangerous to drive a car or use machinery.

■ You must not take ciprofloxacin if you have had problems with your tendons. If you have painful tendons (eg in your ankle) while taking ciprofloxacin, stop taking the medicine and see your doctor.

■ If you are pregnant or breast feeding, you should discuss taking ciprofloxacin with your doctor, as ciprofloxacin is not normally recommended.

■ Tell your doctor if you have epilepsy or if you are taking pain-killers or anti-inflammatory medicines (for example, for arthritis).

Now read the rest of this leaflet. It includes other important information on the safe and effective use of this medicine that might be especially important for you. **This leaflet was last updated on xx/xx/xx**

3   PRESENTING THE BENEFITS OF MEDICINES

One way in which the risks of a treatment can be placed in the context of the potential benefits is to include some general information about how the medicine works. Such extra-statutory information is supported within the legislation through the provisions of article 62 of Council Directive 2001/83/EC. The additional information should be compatible with the Summary of Product Characteristics, useful to the patient and should not be promotional. A few sentences (about 80 words or fewer) should be sufficient to enable the necessary information to be included.

The legal requirements already include a need to describe the pharmacotherapeutic group to which the medicine belongs and the indications for which it is authorised. (Article 59(1)(a) and (b)). This is currently located within the section of the PIL entitled *"What is your medicine and how does it work?".*

This section could also include information on the disease for which the product has been prescribed. The information should be up-to-date, factual, informative and non-promotional. It might include some or all of the following:

- why it is important to treat the disease and what the likely clinical outcome would be if the disease remained untreated;

- whether the treatment is for short term or chronic use;

- whether the medicine is being used to treat the underlying disease (ie curative) or for control of symptoms;

- if the latter, which symptoms will be controlled and how long the effects will last;

- whether the effects will last after the medication is stopped;

- where the medicine is used to treat two or more discrete indications, all should be succinctly described as above;

- where to obtain more information on the condition.

The text should be written in a patient-friendly format and the inclusion of this additional information should be user tested to ensure the revisions generate a balanced opinion of the medicine. Items which are of most relevance to the patient, such as what impact taking the medicine is likely to have on the patient's wellbeing, should be given greatest prominence rather than the mechanism of action of the drug. Prominence can usually be achieved by the use of different sizes of font and spacing of text.

In addition to the details contained within the Summary of Product Characteristics, standard reference texts such as the British National Formulary and the Merck Manual could be used to compile this information. Standard wordings to describe particular conditions are to be encouraged to assist patients to recognise and understand the information presented. Two worked examples are included below.

Example (1)

ANTIHYPERTENSIVE DRUG

WITH BENEFIT INFORMATION

PRODUCT belongs to a group of medicines known as angiotensin II receptor antagonists and is used to treat high blood pressure. High blood pressure often causes no symptoms, but if it is not treated it can damage blood vessels in the long-term. In some cases this can lead to heart attacks, kidney failure, stroke or blindness. That is why it is important not to stop taking this medicine without talking to your doctor.

WITHOUT BENEFIT INFORMATION

PRODUCT belongs to a group of medicines known as angiotensin II receptor antagonists. This medicine lowers your blood pressure.

Example (2)

INHALED STEROID

WITH BENEFIT INFORMATION

PRODUCT contains beclometasone propionate which is one of a group of medicines called corticosteroids, or "steroids". Corticosteroids prevent attacks of asthma by reducing swelling of the air passages and are sometimes called "preventers". You should take this medicine regularly every day even if your asthma is not troubling you. Using PRODUCT can help prevent severe asthma attacks which sometimes need hospital treatment and if left untreated could even be life-threatening.

This medicine should not be used to treat a sudden asthma attack – it will not help. You will need to use a different inhaler ("reliever") to deal with these attacks.

WITHOUT BENEFIT INFORMATION

PRODUCT contains beclometasone propionate which is one of a group of medicines called corticosteroids. These have an anti-inflammatory action and are used to treat asthma.

Presenting information about side effects

4.1   General principles

Patients' understanding and perception of risk is influenced and potentially biased by the manner of presentation of risk and use of statistics in PILs. For example, research has indicated that the use of verbal descriptions corresponding to specific probability ranges (such as "rare" corresponding to <1/1000 but >1/10,0000) has been associated with overestimation and misperception of this risk. Other factors that contribute to difficulty in interpreting risk accurately are:

- inadequate categorisation or description of the side effect (such as lack of information on severity or seriousness);

- the absence of information on baseline risk;

- reference to relative risk instead of absolute risk;

- failure to acknowledge imprecision or uncertainty in risk estimates;

- use of different denominators when comparing risks.

The following principles are designed to maximise the effectiveness of risk communication and minimise misperceptions arising from statistical information in PILs.

Describing side effects: order, seriousness and severity and dose

a. Adverse drug reactions (ADRs) should be grouped in a manner that is meaningful for patients. In particular, grouping should allow easy identification of ADRs that mandate action, such as stopping treatment or seeking medical advice. These data should be provided with estimated risk frequencies (see 4.2 below).

b. Descriptions should convey both the nature and <u>seriousness</u> of possible ADRs. For example, reactions such as gastrointestinal bleeding or rhabdomyolysis can be life-threatening and this should be clear in the PIL. Where possible, symptoms should be provided.

c. Where specific information on the severity of side effects is known this should also be included in the PIL (eg *"headaches that may be severe or long lasting"*).

d. Many side effects are dose-related. PILs should advise patients that higher doses, needed to achieve full benefit/efficacy in some patients, may be associated with an increased risk of side effects. A general warning statement may suffice in some circumstances, but care is needed to ensure that the warning is not alarmist to those who have been prescribed high doses. Specific statements relating to individual side effects may be appropriate if an important dose-relationship exists (eg muscle side effects with statins), or if there is a narrow therapeutic index.

e. Consider providing links/details of further information sources on side effects.

Basic principles of describing statistical risk

f. *Quantifying risk:* present risk numerically using absolute numbers, eg 1 in 10,000 patients. Convey baseline risk and absolute excess risks wherever possible.

g. *Verbal descriptors* (eg "very rare") should only be used if accompanied by the equivalent statistical information. For example, "Very rarely (fewer than 1 in 10,000 patients treated)…"

h. *Point estimates:* convey imprecision of point estimates using terms such as "approximately"/"about"/"around" when referring to estimates for major safety issues (eg *"about 5 extra cancers for every 1000 patients treated"*).

i. *Frequency ranges:* only refer to the upper bound for each range. For example, use *'fewer than 1 in every 1,000'* rather than *'between 1 in 10,000 and 1 in 1,000'.*

j. *Duration of risk:* state the duration over which the excess risk applies if this is known. For example, the risk of agranulocytosis with clozapine is known to differ in the first 18 weeks versus weeks 19-52 and weeks 53 and above. If it is stated in the SPC that specific side effects may occur shortly after starting the drug and are likely to be transient, this information is helpful to include in the PIL.

k. *Frequency estimates based on spontaneous ADR data:* reporting rates are likely to be an underestimate of true incidence or risk. This should be stated in the PIL when referring to data based only on spontaneous ADR data.

l. *Constant denominators:* in some cases, it may be helpful to express the risk of adverse reactions using a 'constant denominator' in presentation of risk frequency, for instance when expressing small differences in risk (see 4.3 below). This will not be appropriate in all circumstances.

4.2   Grouping of side effects (ADRs)

It is particularly important that patients can easily identify the warning symptoms of potentially serious side effects that would necessitate action, such as stopping treatment or needing to seek urgent or immediate medical attention. These side effects and their respective probabilities should therefore be grouped together at the start of the side effect section. The following format is recommended. Advice on necessary actions should be as specific as possible.

"Important side effects or symptoms to look out for – and what to do if you are affected. If you think you may have any of the following side effects or symptoms, stop your medicine and see a doctor as soon as possible". (This wording should be adapted as appropriate to each product).

Examples of side effects that would fall into this category:

- gastrointestinal bleeding or severe gastrointestinal pain with NSAIDs;
- angioedema/facial swelling/serious allergic reactions – any medicine;
- tendon pain with fluoroquinolones;
- unexplained muscle pain with statins;
- abnormal vaginal bleeding or breast lump with HRT;
- warning symptoms of cinchonism with quinine;
- painful swollen leg (possible DVT) with oral contraceptives.

Other possible side effects

In this section, describe the remaining side effects using appropriate lay terms grouped by frequency (most frequent first). Body System Order Class (SOC) grouping should only be used when frequencies are not known/not stated in the SPC.

All PILs should include a statement equivalent to: "Tell your doctor/pharmacist if you get any troublesome symptoms which you think might be side effects."

4.3   Constant denominators

Statistical risks are often presented using a standard numerator of 1 (eg 1 in 1,000 or 1 in 10,000). However, it may be easier in some circumstances to compare these risks when these are presented with the same <u>denominator</u>. The table below shows the three risks presented with a constant numerator (1) and a constant denominator (10,000).

Constant numerator (1)	Constant denominator (10,000)
1 in 10,000	1 in 10,000
1 in 1,000	10 in 10,000
1 in 100	100 in 10,000

The use of a constant denominator may be considered when presenting statistical risk in PILs. This may be particularly useful when expressing small differences or when risks are compared side-by-side (see section 4.4, example 2). The choice of value for constant denominator (ie 10,000, 1000) is flexible and would depend on the data.

Use of constant denominators is not appropriate in all cases and would always require careful user testing to ensure that the information presented is understandable.

Example 1: analgesic product - grouping of ADRs

Possible side effects

Important side effects or symptoms to look out for – and what to do if you are affected

If you think you have any of the following side effects or symptoms, stop your medicine and see a doctor as soon as possible.

The following are rare side effects. They probably affect fewer than 1 in every 1,000 people taking X: severe abdominal pain, vomiting blood or passing black stools (possibly stomach ulcers or bleeding from the intestines).

The following are very rare side effects. They probably affect fewer than 1 in 10,000 people taking X:

- jaundice (yellowing of the skin and eyes) or serious liver problems;

- lower abdominal pain (from inflammation of the colon);

- breathlessness and swollen ankles (due to heart failure);

- swelling of tongue or face (a type of serious allergic reaction);

- worsening of epilepsy;

- severe bleeding or bruising (due to blood disorders);

163

- severe infections (due to low blood cell count);

- severe stiff neck and severe headache (a mild type of meningitis);

- severe skin reactions (with blistering or peeling);

- heart attack (often with severe chest pain);

- stroke or mini-stroke (weakness or loss of sensation or difficulty in speaking).

Other possible side effects

The following are common side effects probably affecting up to 1 in 10 people taking X:

- dizziness, headache, itching, heartburn, abdominal pain or discomfort, diarrhoea, nausea, acid indigestion or swelling of the ankles.

The following are uncommon side effects probably affecting fewer than 1 in 100 people taking X:

- mouth ulcers, vomiting, fatigue, chest pain, depression, difficulty in concentrating, breathlessness, rash, ringing in ears, abdominal distension (bloating), constipation, flatulence ("wind"), difficulty sleeping, cramp or weight gain.

The following are very rare side effects probably affecting fewer than 1 in every 10000 people taking X:

- changes to your menstrual periods, tingling in arms or legs, hair loss, skin reactions to sunlight, anxiety, confusion or blurred vision.

Tell your doctor if you get any troublesome symptoms which you think are side effects.

Example 2: HRT product - absolute risks (baseline and excess), duration of risk, constant denominators and expression of uncertainty

The following example describes the increased risk of stroke and HRT in the context of background absolute risk. The following text is taken from the SPC: *"For women who do not use HRT, it is estimated that the number of cases of stroke that will occur over a 5-year period is about 3 per 1000 women aged 50-59 years and 11 per 1000 women aged 60-69 years. It is estimated that for women who use conjugated oestrogens and MPA for 5 years, the number of additional cases will be between 0 and 3 (best estimate =1) per 1000 users aged 50-59 years and between 1 and 9 (best estimate = 4) per 1000 users aged 60-69 years. It is unknown whether the increased risk also extends to other HRT products".*

This would be translated to the PIL as follows:

For women in their 50s not taking HRT; over a 5-year period, ***about 3* in 1000** are likely to have a stroke.

For women in their 50s taking HRT; over a 5-year period ***about 4* in 1000** are likely to have a stroke, *that is about 1 extra case per 1000 women if using HRT for 5 years.*

For women in their 60s not taking HRT over a 5-year period, ***about 11* in 1000** are likely to have a stroke.

For women in their 60s who are taking HRT, the figure would be ***about 15* in 1000.** *That is about 4 extra cases per 1000 women if using HRT for 5 years.*

If you get:

unexplained migraine-like headaches, with or without disturbed vision – **see a doctor as soon as possible and stop taking HRT** until you have checked with your doctor. These headaches may be an early warning sign of a stroke.
